THORNES
CLASSIC PO

THORNES
CLASSIC POETRY

A Practical Guide for
Key Stage 3

edited by
John Foster and Gordon Dennis

Stanley Thornes (Publishers) Ltd

First published in 1995 by:
Stanley Thornes (Publishers) Ltd
Ellenborough House
Wellington Street
CHELTENHAM GL50 1YW
England

97 98 99 00 / 10 9 8 7 6 5

A catalogue record for this book is available from the British Library.

ISBN 0–7487–1910–5

Typeset by Tech-Set, Gateshead, Tyne & Wear
Printed in Great Britain by T. J. International Ltd., Padstow, Cornwall

Acknowledgements

The editor and publishers wish to thank the following for permission to use copyright material:

HarperCollins Publishers Ltd for 'The Sea' from *Selected Poems* by R.S. Thomas, Collins, 1950;
Penguin Books Ltd for the extract from 'The Miller' from *The Canterbury Tales* by Geoffrey Chaucer, translated by Nevill Coghill (Penguin Classics 1951, Fourth revised edition 1977). Copyright © Nevill Coghill, 1951, 1958, 1960, 1975, 1977;
Random House UK Ltd for 'The Road Not Taken' by Robert Frost from *The Poetry of Robert Frost,* ed. Edward Connery Lathem, Jonathan Cape, 1971;
The Society of Authors, on behalf of The Literary Trustees of Walter de la Mare, for 'The Listeners' by Walter de la Mare from *The Complete Poems of Walter de la Mare*, 1969; and on behalf of the Estate of John Masefield for 'Cargoes' by John Masefield.

'The Vixen' and 'The Badger' by John Clare were taken from *Selected Poems and Prose of John Clare*, chosen and edited by Eric Robinson and Geoffrey Summerfield (Oxford University Press, 1967).

Every effort has been made to trace all the copyright holders, but if any have been inadvertently overlooked the publishers will be pleased to make the necessary arrangement at the first opportunity.

Cover artwork by Russell Thompson
Text artwork by Martin Berry

Contents

Introduction

❧ Creatures ❧

❧ The sea ❧

❧ Mystery and magic ❧

Weathers and seasons

People and places

Reflections

Introduction

Thornes Classic Poetry: A Practical Guide for Key Stage 3 provides a course which is designed to introduce pupils at Key Stage 3 to pre-twentieth-century poetry and to help them to read such poetry with enjoyment and understanding. The poems that have been selected are those which are appropriate to Key Stage 3 pupils in terms of content and language, and the majority of them are by poets who are included in the list of significant poets recommended in the Programmes of Study for Key Stages 3 and 4.

The poems are presented in six sections, each section focusing on a theme appropriate to Key Stage 3. The six sections are: Creatures; The sea; Mystery and magic; Weathers and seasons; People and places; and Reflections. Each poem is introduced in a similar way with background notes providing information about the poet and about the poem. The aim of these notes is first, to introduce the poet by presenting brief interesting biographical details about their life and, second, to provide any essential information about the context in which the poem was written and about relevant features of the poem's content, structure and form. The purpose of these notes is to provide support that will assist the pupil's first reading of the poem. Further support is given in footnotes which gloss unfamiliar words and references.

Following each poem, there are suggestions for activities: either speaking and listening, creative writing or reading and writing. They are designed to develop the pupil's responses and understanding through close textual study, as required by the Programmes of Study. The reading and writing questions are designed to provide an introduction to the more formal approach to literature and to the type of questions pupils may have to answer in tests and examinations. These initial activities are structured so that they lead on to either a piece of creative writing or a spoken outcome. In many cases, the writing suggestion is a poem, in which the pupils are asked to use a technique that they have been exploring in their study of the classic poem. The speaking activity is often the preparation of a reading or presentation of the poem in either pairs or groups. Poems can, therefore, be studied either singly or in groups and the work arising from them can be planned as part of a poetry unit within a National Curriculum scheme of work.

Throughout the book, both in the introductory notes to poems and in the follow-up activities, attention is drawn, as appropriate, to the form and structure of the poem and to any particular features of language that occur within it. Pupils are introduced to forms, such as couplets, sonnets and ballads, and to poetic devices, such as alliteration, simile, metaphor, personification and onomatopoeia. There are clear explanations of each term the first time it appears and cross-references whenever it reappears. To enable pupils to identify that these are technical terms, they are printed in bold at the first occurrence within a context. In addition, other technical terms, such as stress, syllable, etc., which pupils may have difficulty in understanding, are printed in italic and their meaning is given in a glossary at the back of the book.

Creatures

The Eagle

About the poet

Alfred, Lord Tennyson was appointed Poet Laureate by Queen Victoria on the death of William Wordsworth (see p. 80) in 1850. The Poet Laureate is appointed for life and is expected to write poems about important royal occasions, such as weddings and funerals. Tennyson's most famous poems include 'The Lady of Shalott' and 'The Charge of the Light Brigade'. Other poems by Tennyson can be found on pages 3 and 37.

About the poem

This is a short poem, consisting of two verses, each of which has three lines, each one ending with the same rhyme. In the poem Tennyson describes the scene as an eagle watches from a mountainside, then dives on its prey.

The Eagle

He clasps the crag with crooked hands;
Close to the sun in lonely lands,
Ring'd with the azure world, he stands.

The wrinkled sea beneath him crawls;
He watches from his mountain walls,   5
And like the thunderbolt he falls.

ALFRED, LORD TENNYSON
(1809–92)

crag – a steep rugged rock
azure – deep blue

1

Activities

Discuss these questions in pairs, make notes of your answers and then share your ideas in either a group or class discussion.

1. Talk about the first verse. Where is the eagle? What is it doing? Make lists of the words which tell you that

   - the eagle is clinging to the rock
   - how high up the eagle is.

2. Underline the words on each list which start with the same letter or the same two letters. The use of several words starting with the same letter in order to create a particular effect is called **alliteration**. Here are some other examples of alliteration:

   - the whistling wind whipped up the waves
   - in a grim and grimy grotto a grisly ghost grimaced
   - around the rugged rocks the ragged rascal ran
   - in a dark and dingy dungeon the mad magician dwells.

   Think up some examples of your own and write them down.

3. Imagine you had to find a photograph to illustrate the first verse. Discuss what you would look for and make notes of your main ideas.

4. Talk about the second verse. Notice how the action of the final line *contrasts* with the stillness of the scene described in lines 1–5. What is the eagle compared with in the last line? Can you suggest another word to describe how swiftly the eagle falls?

5. Either look for suitable pictures in old copies of magazines that you could use to form a background for the text and create a poster using the text and the pictures or copy out the text and illustrate it yourself.

Write your own six-line poem describing an animal which is about to pounce on its prey. Start by describing the animal and what it is doing as it watches and waits. Try to provide a contrast, as Tennyson does, between the stillness of the scene before the animal strikes and the sudden action as it pounces. You could use a *comparison* to describe how it strikes. Do not worry about making it rhyme, unless you would like to do so.

The Owl

About the poem

This poem presents a picture of an owl at daybreak at two different times of the year. The poem consists of two verses of seven lines and both verses have the same pattern. One line in each verse is repeated and the last two lines of each verse are the same.

The Owl

When cats run home and light is come,
 And dew is cold upon the ground,
And the far-off stream is dumb,
 And the whirring sail goes round,
 And the whirring sail goes round;   5
  Alone and warming his five wits,
  The white owl in the belfry sits.

When merry milkmaids click the latch,
 And rarely smells the new-mown hay,
And the cock hath sung beneath the thatch   10
 Twice or thrice his roundelay,
 Twice or thrice his roundelay;
  Alone and warming his five wits,
  The white owl in the belfry sits.

ALFRED, LORD TENNYSON
(1809–92)

belfry – bell-tower
rarely – greatly
roundelay – repetitive song

Activities

Reading and writing   Read the poem, then write answers to these questions.

1. What time of year is described in the first verse? List the words and phrases which tell you what time of year it is.

2. What time of year is described in the second verse? List the words and phrases which tell you what time of year it is.

3. The last two lines of each verse are the same. What is the owl doing? What does this repetition suggest about the owl?

Speaking and listening   This is a poem with a strong rhythm. In pairs, discuss how you could read it aloud together, then try doing so. Decide what effect you would want your reading of it to tell the listener. Practise reading it through then either tape-record a reading of it or present your reading of it to the rest of the class.

Creative writing   Write your own poem about the behaviour of an animal at a particular time of day – for example, early in the evening as darkness falls or in the middle of the night. Before you begin, hold a class discussion in which you share stories of how you have seen animals behaving at particular times. Talk about how your pets behave and how you have seen animals behaving either in the wild or in zoos. You could try to write two verses and to make use of repetition to show what the animal does. For example, a tiger walking up and down its cage in a zoo, while waiting for feeding time; a dog impatiently waiting for its afternoon walk.

The Vixen

About the poet

John Clare was a Northamptonshire labourer. His poems are about the animals and countryside around his home.

About the poem

In this poem Clare describes how a vixen (a female fox) looks after her cubs. Like many of Clare's poems it is written in pairs of lines which rhyme. A pair of lines which rhyme is called a **rhyming couplet**. For example:

She snuffs and barks if any passes <u>by</u>
And swings her tail and turns prepared to <u>fly</u>.

The Vixen

Among the taller wood with ivy hung,
The old fox plays and dances round her young.
She snuffs and barks if any passes by
And swings her tail and turns prepared to fly.
The horseman hurries by, she bolts to see,   5
And turns agen, from danger never free.
If any stands she runs among the poles
And barks and snaps and drives them in the holes.
The shepherd sees them and the boy goes by
And gets a stick and progs the hole to try.   10
They get all still and lie in safety sure,
And out again when everything's secure,
And start and snap at blackbirds bouncing by
To fight and catch the great white butterfly.

JOHN CLARE
(1793–1864)

bolts – darts quickly
agen – again
poles – small trees
progs – prods

Activities

Speaking and listening

Consider these questions in groups, then share your ideas in a whole class discussion.

1. What do you learn from the poem about how the vixen looks after her cubs?

2. What does the poem tell you about the cubs and how they behave?

3. Discuss the picture which Clare gives of the vixen. Choose the words from the list below which best describe the impression he creates. Discuss the reasons for your choices:

- playful
- watchful
- caring
- energetic
- cunning
- anxious
- protective
- fearful
- daring.

4. Which lines do you think create the clearest picture of

- the vixen
- the fox cubs?

Creative writing   Write a poem which describes a mother animal looking after her young. After you have chosen your animal you could look for pictures and read about how the animal cares for its young in books from the non-fiction section in the library. Before you begin, decide what impression you want your poem to give of the animal and of her young. You could try to write your poem in rhyming couplets.

Badger

About the poet

For details of John Clare see page 4.

About the poem

This poem, like 'The Vixen', is written in **rhyming couplets** (see p. 4).

ꞋꞋꞋ Badger ꞋꞋꞋ

When midnight comes a host of dogs and men
Go out and track the badger to his den,
And put a sack within the hole, and lie
Till the old grunting badger passes by.
He comes and hears – they let the strongest loose.   5
The old fox hears the noise and drops the goose.
The poacher shoots and hurries from the cry,
And the old hare half wounded buzzes by.
They get a forkēd stick to bear him down
And clap the dogs and take him to the town,   10
And bait him all the day with many dogs,
And laugh and shout and fright the scampering hogs.
He runs along and bites at all he meets:
They shout and hollo down the noisy streets.

He turns about to face the loud uproar   15
And drives the rebels to their very door.
The frequent stone is hurled where'er they go;
When badgers fight, then every one's a foe.
The dogs are clapt and urged to join the fray;
The badger turns and drives them all away.   20
Though scarcely half as big, dimute and small,
He fights with dogs for hours and beats them all.
The heavy mastiff, savage in the fray,
Lies down and licks his feet and turns away.
The bulldog knows his match and waxes cold,   25
The badger grins and never leaves his hold.
He drives the crowd and follows at their heels
And bites them through – the drunkard swears and reels.

The frighted women take the boys away,
The blackguard laughs and hurries on the fray.   30
He tries to reach the woods, an awkward race,
But sticks and cudgels quickly stop the chase.
He turns agen and drives the noisy crowd
And beats the many dogs in noises loud.
He drives away and beats them every one,   35
And then they loose them all and set them on.
He falls as dead and kicked by boys and men,
Then starts and grins and drives the crowd agen;
Till kicked and torn and beaten out he lies
And leaves his hold, and cackles, groans, and dies.   40

JOHN CLARE
(1793–1864)

clapt – urged on by clapping
dimute – grown smaller
mastiff – large, powerful dog
waxes – becomes

reels – staggers
blackguard – villain
cudgels – short, thick wooden sticks
agen – again

Activities

Speaking and listening Discuss these questions in groups, then share your ideas in a class discussion.

1. Talk about what happens in the poem. The main action of the poem can be divided into five sections: lines 1–8; lines 9–14; lines 15–26; lines 27–30; and lines 31–40. Go through the poem and discuss what happens in each section.

2. What do you feel about the way the people treat the badger?

3. How does Clare feel about the badger? Does he

    - admire it
    - dislike it
    - feel sorry for it
    - not care about what happens to it?

Find evidence from the poem to support your view.

Reading and writing

Look again at each of the five sections of the poem. Write one or two sentences in your own words to sum up what is happening in each section, then use these as the basis for writing your own version of the badger's story. You could imagine you are the badger and describe its thoughts and feelings.

Draw a picture-strip of eight to ten frames based on what happens in the poem. Choose suitable lines from the poem to use as captions for each of your pictures.

From 'Windsor Forest'

About the poet

Throughout his life, Alexander Pope suffered from ill-health. As a result of a childhood illness, he was very short, never growing above 4ft 6in. Pope often used his poems to present arguments or to poke fun at fashionable society.

About the poem

These lines, which Pope wrote when he was 16, are taken from a longer poem called 'Windsor Forest'. Pope uses this section to present his views on hunting and shooting. The poem is written in **rhyming couplets** (see p. 4).

From 'Windsor Forest'

See! from the brake the whirring pheasant springs,
And mounts exulting on triumphant wings:
Short is his joy; he feels the fiery wound,
Flutters in blood, and panting beats the ground.
Ah! what avail his glossy, varying dyes,   5
His purple crest, and scarlet-circled eyes,
The vivid green his shining plumes unfold,
His painted wings, and breast that flames with gold?
    Nor yet, when moist *Arcturus* clouds the sky,
The woods and fields their pleasing toils deny.   10
To plains with well-breathed beagles we repair,
And trace the mazes of the circling hare.
(Beasts, taught by us, their fellow beasts pursue,
And learn of man each other to undo.)
With slaught'ring guns th' unwearyed fowler roves,   15
When frosts have whitened all the naked groves;
Where doves in flocks the leafless trees o'ershade,
And lonely woodcocks haunt the wat'ry glade.
He lifts the tube, and levels with his eye;
Straight a short thunder breaks the frozen sky.   20
Oft, as in airy rings they skim the heath,
The clam'rous plovers feel the leaden death:
Oft, as the mounting larks their notes prepare,
They fall, and leave their little lives in air.

ALEXANDER POPE
(1688–1744)

brake – clump of bushes
Arcturus – star seen on September mornings
tube – gun
clam'rous – noisy and loud

Activities

Reading and writing

Read the poem, then write answers to these questions.

1. Make a list of words that Pope uses to describe

   - the pheasant's movements (lines 1–2)
   - its colours (lines 5–8).

2. Which words does Pope use to put across the idea of the pheasant's sudden, violent death (lines 3–4)?

3. What is Pope's view of shooting pheasants? Support your answer by referring to the poem.

4. What is Pope's view of hare-coursing (hunting hares with beagles)? Pick out the lines which tell you what his views are.

5. What is Pope's view of shooting birds, such as woodcocks, plovers and larks? List the words and phrases in lines 15–24 which tell you what his view is.

Creative writing

Write a short poem which expresses your views on hunting or shooting by describing an incident in which an animal is killed or narrowly escapes death.

Bats!

About the poet

D.H. Lawrence was the son of a miner. Before becoming a full-time writer, he worked for two years as a teacher. He then travelled widely, living for a time in a number of different countries, including Italy, France, Australia, Mexico and the USA. In addition to poetry and short stories, he wrote novels such as *Sons and Lovers* and *Women in Love*.

About the poem

In this extract from a longer poem, 'Bat', D.H. Lawrence describes how he feels about bats.

🌿 Bats! 🌿

Creatures that hang themselves up like an old rag, to sleep;
And disgustingly upside down.
Hanging upside down like rows of disgusting old rags
And grinning in their sleep.
Bats!

In China the bat is a symbol of happiness.

Not for me!

D.H. LAWRENCE
(1885–1930)

Activities

Speaking and listening Discuss these questions in pairs, make notes of your answers and then share them in a group or class discussion.

1. Discuss how D.H. Lawrence feels about bats. Pick out the words and phrases which tell you how he feels.

2. In this poem Lawrence uses a comparison to help him to tell us how he feels about bats. He says that when they are hanging upside down, they look 'like rows of disgusting old rags'. A comparison which is made by using 'like' or 'as' is called a **simile**. Here are some other examples of similes:

   • The shark's teeth are like a row of daggers
   • The thunder was like a bomb exploding
   • Her face was as red as a beetroot
   • He is as cunning as an old fox.

   Think up some examples of your own and write them down. Further work on similes can be found following the poem 'An emerald is as green as grass' on page 106.

Creative writing Work with a partner. Choose an animal and write down words you could use to describe

- its face and its head – its ears, eyes, nose, mouth and teeth
- its body – its arms, legs, claws and tail
- its hair or its skin.

Then try to think of some similes to describe one or two of its features. Think also about how it moves and the noises it makes. What does it move like? What do the noises it makes sound like?

Use your ideas to draft a poem about the animal in which you include some similes.

A narrow Fellow in the Grass

About the poet

Emily Dickinson was an American poet. She wrote about 1 800 poems, but only seven of them were published during her lifetime. She liked being on her own and during her forties she began to spend more and more time alone in her own room. She wore only white and rarely came downstairs.

About the poem

In this poem, Emily Dickinson imagines how a boy feels whenever he meets a snake. Notice the punctuation of the poem: it is unusual because of the way the poet uses capital letters for certain words and dashes rather than other punctuation marks. The dashes act as punctuation marks, rather than as breaks in the poet's thoughts, and show you when to pause when you are reading the poem aloud. Another poem by Emily Dickinson can be found on page 120.

A narrow Fellow in the Grass

A narrow Fellow in the Grass
Occasionally rides –
You may have met Him – did you not
His notice sudden is –

The Grass divides as with a Comb –   5
A spotted shaft is seen –
And then it closes at your feet
And opens further on –

He likes a Boggy Acre   10
A Floor too cool for Corn –
Yet when a Boy, and Barefoot –
I more than once at Noon
Have passed, I thought, a Whip lash
Unbraiding in the Sun   15
When stooping to secure it
It wrinkled, and was gone –

Several of Nature's People
I know, and they know me –
I feel for them a transport   20
Of cordiality –

But never met this Fellow
Attended, or alone
Without a tighter breathing
And Zero at the Bone –

EMILY DICKINSON
(1830–86)

Unbraiding – untwisting

Activities

Speaking and
listening Discuss these questions in groups. Appoint a secretary to
take notes of your ideas, then share them in a class
discussion.

1. Here are some statements about what the poem says.
   Talk about each statement in turn and find the words
   and phrases which the poet uses to express these ideas:

   - you often come across snakes suddenly
   - you catch a glimpse of a snake, then it disappears
     again

- snakes like cool, damp places
- when a snake is lying still, you can easily mistake it for something else
- there is something sinister and frightening about the snake.

2. Discuss what the boy in the poem feels about snakes. Pick out the words and phrases in lines 21–4 which tell you how he feels. What are your feelings about snakes? In what ways are they the same as, or different from, the boy's feelings?

3. Talk about the unusual way that Emily Dickinson uses capital letters. Does it help you to read and understand the poem because it draws your attention to particular words or do you find it odd and puzzling?

Creative writing Write your own poem about a creature which you find sinister or frightening. Try to describe an incident or incidents when it has given you a fright and what it is about the creature that frightens you. You could experiment with using capitals in an unusual way to draw attention to particular words.

Write a poem about an animal in which the first letters of each line together spell the animal's name down the page. A poem which spells a word in this way is called an **acrostic**. Here is an acrostic about a cat:

Creeps stealthily in the fence's shadow
Alert, watchful
Terrorist waiting to pounce.

The Gallows

About the poet

Edward Thomas was killed in action during the First World War. All his poetry was written during the last two-and-a-half years of his life. Many of his poems are sad and are about nature and the countryside.

About the poem

This poem is about the animals a gamekeeper kills and what he does with their bodies.

The Gallows

There was a weasel lived in the sun
With all his family,
Till a keeper shot him with his gun
And hung him up on a tree,
Where he swings in the wind and rain,   5
In the sun and in the snow,
Without pleasure, without pain,
On the dead oak tree bough.

There was a crow who was no sleeper,
But a thief and a murderer   10
Till a very late hour; and this keeper
Made him one of the things that were,
To hang and flap in rain and wind,
In the sun and in the snow.
There are no more sins to be sinned   15
On the dead oak tree bough.

There was a magpie, too,
Had a long tongue and a long tail;
He could both talk and do –
But what did that avail?   20
He, too, flaps in the wind and rain
Alongside weasel and crow,
Without pleasure, without pain,
On the dead oak tree bough.

And many other beasts
And birds, skin, bone and feather,   25
Have been taken from their feasts
And hung up there together,
To swing and have endless leisure
In the sun and in the snow,   30
Without pain, without pleasure,
On the dead oak tree bough.

EDWARD THOMAS
(1878–1917)

avail – help

Activities

Speaking and listening Discuss these questions in groups. Make notes of your views and then share them in a class discussion.

1. Make a list of the animals which the keeper kills. Talk about why he kills them. Which lines tell you why he kills them?

2. What does the keeper do with the animals' bodies? Discuss why he puts them there.

3. What is a gallows? Find out what a gallows is, then discuss why the poem is called 'The Gallows'.

4. Look at the last four lines of each verse. Which line is the same in all four verses? Which lines are the same in three of the four verses? Pick out the words in these lines which help to suggest that the animals have been executed for their crimes.

5. How do you feel about what the gamekeeper does? How does the poet feel? Which lines tell you how he feels?

In groups, prepare a reading of the poem. Talk about the effect you want your reading to have on your listeners, then discuss ways of dividing the poem up, so that some lines are read by one person and other lines are read by pairs or groups. Try out different ways of reading the poem, then either tape-record your reading or present it to the rest of the class. You could choose a piece of music to fade in and out as a background to your reading. What kind of music would you choose? What effect would you want the music to create?

Upon the Snail

About the poet

John Bunyan's most famous book is *The Pilgrim's Progress*, which has been translated into over a hundred languages and was widely used as a text in schools during the eighteenth and nineteenth centuries. He was a preacher and spent twelve years in jail for holding unlawful meetings.

About the poem

In this poem, which is a **parable**, (see p. 54), Bunyan describes how a snail behaves in order to make a comment about how humans should behave.

Upon the Snail

She goes but softly, but she goeth sure;
    She stumbles not as stronger creatures do:
Her journey's shorter, so she may endure
    Better than they which do much further go.

She makes no noise, but stilly seizeth on   5
    The flower or herb appointed for her food,
The which she quietly doth feed upon,
    While others range, and gare, but find no good.

And though she doth but very softly go,
    However, 'tis not fast, nor slow, but sure;   10
And certainly they that do travel so,
    The prize they do aim at, they do procure.

JOHN BUNYAN
(1628–88)

stilly – silently
herb – grass
gare – stare about
procure – obtain

Activities

Speaking and listening   Discuss these questions in pairs. Make notes of your ideas, then share your views in either a group or class discussion.

1. Talk about the first verse. Pick out the words and phrases in lines 1 and 2 which tell you how the snail moves. What do they suggest about the snail's pace? How does its pace help it to complete its journey?

2. Discuss the second verse. What does it tell you about the snail's eating habits? How are they different from those of other creatures?

3. Talk about the third verse:

   - what does Bunyan say about the snail and its progress in lines 9 and 10?

- what does he say about how people behave in lines 11 and 12?
- what is the *moral* of the poem?

Talk about how the *pace* of the poem is like the snail's pace. In pairs, take it in turns to read the poem aloud. See who is the most successful at bringing out the poem's pace.

Creative writing
Stories about animals are often used to make a comment on human behaviour and are called **fables** (e.g., in *Aesop's Fables*). Use the library to find one of *Aesop's Fables* and retell it in your own words as either a poem or a story; or make up a poem or a story which is a fable. You could illustrate your work and collect your poems and stories into a class book of fables.

The Tyger

About the poet

William Blake worked as an engraver, producing illustrations for many books, including his own books of poems. His books were never popular during his life and he died poor. His most famous poems are 'The Tyger' and 'Jerusalem'.

About the poem

This poem is about the creation of the tiger. The poet is wondering about the nature of its creator. The poem is written in verses of four lines and each verse has the same pattern of rhymes. The pattern of rhymes in a verse or a poem is called the **rhyme scheme**. You can describe the rhyme scheme of a verse by giving each new rhyme a letter of the alphabet. In the first verse of 'The Tyger' the first and second lines rhyme and the third and fourth lines rhyme, so the rhyme scheme is *aabb*.

Tyger! Tyger! burning bright	a	these two
In the forests of the night,	a	lines rhyme
What immortal hand or eye	b	these two
Could frame thy fearful symmetry?	b	lines rhyme

The Tyger

Tyger! Tyger! burning bright
In the forests of the night,
What immortal hand or eye
Could frame thy fearful symmetry?

In what distant deeps or skies
Burned the fire of thine eyes?
On what wings dare he aspire?
What the hand dare seize the fire?

And what shoulder, and what art,
Could twist the sinews of thy heart?
And, when thy heart began to beat,
What dread hand? And what dread feet?

What the hammer? What the chain?
In what furnace was thy brain?
What the anvil? What dread grasp
Dare its deadly terrors clasp?

When the stars threw down their spears,
And watered heaven with their tears,
Did he smile his work to see?
Did he who made the Lamb make thee?

Tyger! Tyger! burning bright
In the forests of the night,
What immortal hand or eye
Dare frame thy fearful symmetry?

WILLIAM BLAKE
(1757–1827)

sinews – muscles

Activities

In pairs, read and discuss these questions, then write
answers to them.

1. What impression of the tiger do you get from the first
   verse? What does the word 'burning' suggest about the
   tiger? What does the phrase 'fearful symmetry' suggest?

2. In verses 2, 3 and 4 Blake asks a series of questions about
   how the tiger was created. Pick out the words and
   phrases which suggest that the tiger is

   * powerful and strong
   * dangerous and terrifying.

3. The questions which Blake asks in verse 5 are different
   from the questions in the first four verses. Why does
   Blake wonder whether the tiger's creator also created the
   Lamb? What qualities does the Lamb have which are so
   different from the qualities of the tiger? Why does he
   ask 'Did he smile?'

4. Notice how the final verse is almost the same as the first
   verse. What is the effect of replacing 'could' with 'dare'?
   What does the word 'dare' suggest?

5. How would you describe the poet's feelings about the tiger
   and its creation? Which of these words sums up his feelings:

   * astonishment
   * terror
   * awe
   * surprise
   * bewilderment?

   Give reasons for your answer.

6. Look again at the rhyme scheme of the first verse. Can
   you write down the rhyme scheme of the other verses in
   the poem?

7. Work out the rhyme scheme for Tennyson's poem 'The
   Owl' and any other poems of your choice.

Notice how Blake uses the rhythm of the poem to help him
emphasise the words which suggest what type of creature
the tiger is. In groups, prepare a reading of the poem. Before
you begin, go through the poem verse by verse and work
out where the *stresses* come by underlining which *syllables*
are stressed. Here are the stresses for the first verse:

> Tyger! Tyger! burning bright
> In the forests of the night,
> What immortal hand or eye
> Could frame thy fearful symmetry?

The sea

The Sea

22

The Sea

They wash their hands in it.
The salt turns to soap
In their hands. Wearing it
At their wrists, they make bracelets
Of it; it runs in beads
On their jackets. A child's
Plaything? It has hard whips
That it cracks, and knuckles
To pummel you. It scrubs
And scours; it chews rocks
To sand; its embraces
Leave you without breath. Mostly
It is a stomach, where bones,
Wrecks, continents are digested.

R.S. THOMAS
(1913–)

Handwritten annotations: wading hands with dangling; on picnic; crystalizes?; stick hands in up to wrist?; 2 ideas connected — jewellery, swinging arms (why wearing jackets?); skin — slightly only; the thing the children do with the sea — move hands through — is like movement of washing → ∴ salt is seen as soap in water; a thing which makes the water unclear like soap?; pummel; hold you under water longer than you want to be; ships; ie wears them away; charge; person — waves; in round movement of waves; when ya get caught in a wave or current; takes bites out of them; 5; 10

Activities

Speaking and listening

In pairs, discuss these questions, then share your ideas with another pair in a group discussion.

1. What is the sea compared with in lines 2, 4 and 5? What do these comparisons suggest about the sea?

2. What is the sea compared with in lines 7–11? What different view of the sea do these lines suggest? *[ogre, means mother]*

3. What comparison is made in lines 13 and 14? How does this suggest that the sea is powerful and dangerous? *[human stomach, acid — can eat huge things]*

4. Suggest other comparisons that Thomas might have used in order to describe the sea as
   - calm and gentle *[rocking like a cradle]*
   - fierce and dangerous. *[like a car wash, storm, volcano]*

Creative writing

Write your own poem about the moods of the sea. To help you get started, you could listen to a piece of music which represents the sea: for example, *A Sea Symphony* by Vaughan Williams. As you listen to the music jot down words and ideas, then use some of them to start drafting your poem.

On the Sea

About the poet

For details of John Keats see page 43.

About the poem

This poem was written on 17 April 1817, while the poet was staying on the Isle of Wight. The poem is a sonnet. Keats describes different features of the sea and how relaxing he finds it to sit watching and listening to the sea.

A **sonnet** is a poem with fourteen lines, each of which usually has ten *syllables* and the same basic pattern of stressed and unstressed syllables. Some sonnets, such as 'On the Sea', consist of an eight-line section (the octave), followed by a six-line section (the sestet). Sonnets can have a variety of different **rhyme schemes** (see p. 19). The rhyme scheme can be described by giving each new rhyme the next letter of the alphabet. Thus, the complete rhyme scheme of 'On the Sea' can be described as *abba abba cde dec*. Further examples of sonnets can be found on pages 53 and 91.

On the Sea

It keeps eternal whisperings around
   Desolate shores, and with its mighty swell
   Gluts twice ten thousand caverns; till the spell
Of Hecate leaves them their old shadowy sound.
Often 'tis in such gentle temper found   5
   That scarcely will the very smallest shell
   Be mov'd for days from where it sometime fell,
When last the winds of heaven were unbound.
Oh ye who have your eye-balls vex'd and tir'd,
   Feast them upon the wideness of the sea;   10
     Oh ye whose ears are dinn'd with uproar rude,
   Or fed too much with cloying melody –
     Sit ye near some old cavern's mouth and brood
Until ye start, as if the sea-nymphs quir'd!

JOHN KEATS
(1795–1821)

Gluts – fills up	*start* – are startled
Hecate – goddess of the moon	*quir'd* – sang
vex'd – strained	

Activities

Speaking and listening

In pairs, discuss questions 1–3.

1. Talk about the pictures of the sea that Keats presents in the first eight lines. What picture does he present in

   - lines 1–2
   - lines 2–4
   - lines 5–8?

2. Discuss what you would be feeling if your eye-balls were 'vex'd and tir'd' (line 9) or your ears were 'dinn'd with uproar rude' (line 11). What does Keats suggest you could do to make yourself feel better (lines 13–14)?

3. Study the picture opposite. Discuss what the person might be thinking and feeling as she stares out to sea. Make lists of words to describe
   - the things she sees
   - the sounds she hears
   - the things she can smell.

Creative writing

Write a poem describing the thoughts and feelings of the person as she stares out to sea. Use words and phrases from your lists (above) to help you get started.

Cargoes

About the poet

At the age of 13, John Masefield joined the Merchant Navy. During his second voyage, he left the ship in New York and took a job as a bartender. He then worked in a carpet factory, before returning to England to become a writer. As well as poetry, he wrote novels, plays and books for children, such as *The Box of Delights*. From 1930 to 1967, he was Poet Laureate.

About the poem

In this poem, Masefield describes three different types of ship and the cargoes they carry. The poem is written in five-line verses with varying rhythms which help to show the different ways the ships move.

Cargoes

Quinquereme of Nineveh from distant Ophir
Rowing home to haven in sunny Palestine
With a cargo of ivory,
And apes and peacocks,
Sandalwood, cedarwood, and sweet white wine.   5

Stately Spanish galleon coming from the Isthmus,
Dipping through the Tropics by the palm-green shores,
With a cargo of diamonds,
Emeralds, amethysts,
Topazes, and cinnamon, and gold moidores.   10

Dirty British coaster with a salt-caked smoke stack
Butting through the Channel in the mad March days,
With a cargo of Tyne coal,
Road-rail, pig-lead,
Firewood, iron-ware, and cheap tin trays.   15

JOHN MASEFIELD
(1878–1967)

Quinquereme – a ship with five banks of oars
Ophir – a mysterious land where traders went in biblical times
Nineveh – ancient city on the River Tigris in Mesopotamia
Isthmus – Isthmus of Panama in Central America
moidores – gold coins

Activities

Speaking and listening   Discuss these questions in groups and then prepare a reading of the poem to give to the rest of the class.

1. Discuss the impression of the quinquereme and how it moves. What is suggested

   - by the words 'rowing', 'haven' and 'sunny' (line 2)
   - by the description of its cargo?

2. What impression of the Spanish galleon and how it moves is given

   - by the words 'stately' (line 6) and 'dipping' (line 7)
   - by the description of its cargo?

3. What impression of the British coaster and how it moves is given

   - by the words 'dirty' (line 11), 'salt-caked smoke stack' (line 11) and 'butted' (line 12)
   - the description of its cargo?

4. Talk about how Masefield uses the rhythm of each verse to suggest the way the ships move and to bring out the contrast between the smoothness of the quinquereme and the stateliness of the Spanish galleon with their rich, exotic cargoes and the slowness of the British coaster with its heavy industrial cargo. Work together to produce a reading of the poem which conveys these contrasts.

Creative writing In pairs, try to write an extra verse for the poem about another type of ship (e.g., an oil tanker, a trawler, a cross-Channel ferry, a freighter). Before you begin, decide what impression you want to give of the ship and how it moves and make a list of words you could use to give that impression. Then, as you write your verse, try to create a rhythm which suggests the way that type of ship moves.

Song of the Galley-slaves

About the poet

For details about Rudyard Kipling see page 58.

About the poem

This poem is a chant which gradually gathers *pace*. The chant begins as if it is a plea for freedom, but ends on a note of defiance.

✇ *Song of the Galley-slaves* ✇

We pulled for you when the wind was against us and the sails were low.
　　Will you never let us go?
We ate bread and onions when you took towns, or ran aboard quickly
　　when you were beaten back by the foe.
The Captains walked up and down the deck in fair weather singing　　5
　　songs, but we were below.
We fainted with our chins on the oars and you did not see that we were
　　idle, for we still swung to and fro.
　　Will you never let us go?
The salt made the oar-handles like shark-skin; our knees were cut to　　10
　　the bone with salt-cracks; our hair was stuck to our foreheads; and
　　our lips were cut to the gums, and you whipped us because we could
　　not row.
　　Will you never let us go?
But, in a little time, we shall run out of the port-holes as the water　　15
　　runs along the oar-blade, and though you tell the others to row after
　　us you will never catch us till you catch the oar-thresh and tie up the
　　winds in the belly of the sail. Aho!
　　Will you never let us go?　　　　　　　　　　　　　　　　20

RUDYARD KIPLING
(1865–1936)

oar-thresh – water washed up by the oars

Activities

Speaking and listening　　In pairs, study these statements about what the galley-slaves say in their song. Discuss each statement in turn. Find the lines which express these ideas and the words and phrases which are used to put them across:

- we've rowed for you in all sorts of places, in all kinds of weathers
- we've kept going no matter how we've felt
- you didn't care what happened to us
- our bodies have suffered
- you will kill us, but you won't break our spirit.

In groups, prepare a presentation of the poem. Try to bring out the slaves' tiredness and to show the chant beginning with a note of pleading and ending on a note of defiance.

Creative writing   Use the ideas presented in the poem and what you imagine it must have been like for galley-slaves to develop your own song of the galley-slaves. Try to use rhythm and repetition to express how they feel about their situation and how tiring and boring their work is. Here is the start of such a song:

> We pulled for you in the wind and the rain.
>   To and fro, to and fro.
> Again and again, Again and again.
>   Will you never let us go?

Write some more verses to add to this song or invent a song of your own.

The Inchcape Rock

About the poet

Robert Southey was expelled from Westminster School for writing an essay against flogging. He was a friend of Samuel Taylor Coleridge (see p. 49) and William Wordsworth (see p. 80) and was Poet Laureate from 1813 to 1843.

About the poem

The Inchcape Rock is a rocky reef in the North Sea, about 12 miles from the Scottish town of Arbroath. The Abbot of Arbroath fixed a bell to a timber float to warn sailors where the reef was. The poem is a **ballad** – a poem or song telling a well-known story – written in four-line verses which have the **rhyme scheme** (see p. 19) *aabb*.

ॠ *The Inchcape Rock* ॠ

1 The Inchcape Bell

No stir in the air, no stir in the sea,
The ship was still as she could be,
Her sails from heaven received no motion,
Her keel was steady in the ocean.

Without either sign or sound of their shock 5
The waves flowed over the Inchcape Rock;
So little they rose, so little they fell,
They did not move the Inchcape Bell.

The Abbot of Aberbrothok
Had placed that bell on the Inchcape Rock; 10
On a buoy in the storm it floated and swung,
And over the waves its warning rung.

When the Rock was hid by the surge's swell,
The mariners heard the warning bell;
And then they knew the perilous Rock, 15
And blessed the Abbot of Aberbrothok.

2 Sir Ralph the Rover's wicked deed

The sun in heaven was shining gay,
All things were joyful on that day;
The sea-birds screamed as they wheeled round,
And there was joyaunce in their sound. 20

The buoy of the Inchcape Bell was seen
A darker speck on the ocean green;
Sir Ralph the Rover walked his deck,
And he fixed his eye on the darker speck.

He felt the cheering power of spring; 25
It made him whistle, it made him sing;
His heart was mirthful to excess,
But the Rover's mirth was wickedness.

His eye was on the Inchcape float;
Quoth he, 'My men, put out the boat, 30
And row me to the Inchcape Rock,
And I'll plague the Abbot of Aberbrothok.'

The boat is lowered, the boatmen row,
And to the Inchcape Rock they go;
Sir Ralph bent over from the boat, 35
And he cut the Bell from the Inchcape float.

Down sunk the Bell with a gurgling sound,
The bubbles rose and burst around;
Quoth Sir Ralph, 'The next who comes to the Rock
Won't bless the Abbot of Aberbrothok.' 40

3 Sir Ralph the Rover's return

Sir Ralph the Rover sailed away,
He scoured the seas for many a day;
And now grown rich with plundered store,
He steers his course for Scotland's shore.

So thick a haze o'erspreads the sky   45
They cannot see the sun on high;
The wind hath blown a gale all day,
At evening it hath died away.

On the deck the Rover takes his stand,
So dark it is they see no land.   50
Quoth Sir Ralph, 'It will be lighter soon,
For there is the dawn of the rising Moon.'

'Canst hear,' said one, 'the breakers roar?
For methinks we should be near the shore.'
'Now where we are I cannot tell,   55
But I wish I could hear the Inchcape Bell.'

They hear no sound, the swell is strong;
Though the wind hath fallen, they drift along,
Till the vessel strikes with a shivering shock, –
'Oh Christ! it is the Inchcape Rock!'   60

Sir Ralph the Rover tore his hair;
He cursed himself in his despair;
The waves rush in on every side,
The ship is sinking beneath the tide.

But even in his dying fear   65
One dreadful sound could the Rover hear,
A sound as if with the Inchcape Bell
The Devil below was ringing his knell.

ROBERT SOUTHEY
(1774–1843)

ව ව

Aberbrothok – Arbroath
surge's swell – large waves rising
joyaunce – enjoyment

mirthful – full of laughter
Quoth – said
knell – sound of a funeral bell

Activities

Reading and writing

Read the poem, then write answers to these questions.

1. What do you learn about the Inchcape Rock and the Inchcape Bell from

   - verses 1 and 2
   - verses 3 and 4?

2. What mood is created at the start of the second section (verse 5)? How is it different from the mood created by the first two verses of the poem?

3. Why did Sir Ralph cut the bell off?

4. How did Sir Ralph become the victim of his own wickedness?

5. Which lines in section 3 tell you that Sir Ralph regretted what he had done?

6. What sound does Sir Ralph hear as he is dying? Why is it 'dreadful' (verse 17)?

7. What is the *moral* of the poem?

Speaking and listening

Imagine that one of Sir Ralph the Rover's crew miraculously survived. In pairs, role-play a scene in which a reporter interviews him and asks him what happened and how he feels about what Sir Ralph did.

Divide the class into three groups and prepare a reading of the poem, with each group reading one of the three sections. In your group, decide what mood you want your reading to create and try to produce a reading which brings out the contrasting moods of the three sections.

Creative writing

Use the library to find and read other ballads about the sea, such as 'Sir Patrick Spens'. Then try to write your own ballad telling a story of the sea. You could base it on a well-known story, such as the story of Grace Darling, or a relevant news item (e.g., about a tanker running aground or the experiences of one of the boat people, such as the refugees who tried to flee in small boats from Cuba to the USA in autumn 1994).

The Three Fishers

The Three Fishers

Three fishers went sailing away to the West,
    Away to the West as the sun went down;
Each thought on the woman who loved him the best,
    And the children stood watching them out of the town:
For men must work, and women must weep,   5
And there's little to earn, and many to keep,
    Though the harbour-bar be moaning.

Three wives sat up in the lighthouse tower,
    And they trimmed the lamps as the sun went down;
And they looked at the squall, and they looked at the shower,   10
    And the night-rack came rolling up ragged and brown:
But men must work, and women must weep,
Though storms be sudden, and waters deep,
    And the harbour-bar be moaning.

Three corpses lay out on the shining sands   15
   In the morning gleam as the tide went down,
And the women are weeping and wringing their hands
   For those who will never come back to the town.
For men must work, and women must weep,
And the sooner it's over, the sooner to sleep,   20
   And goodbye to the bar and its moaning.

CHARLES KINGSLEY
(1819–75)

harbour-bar – bank of sand across a harbour mouth
squall – sudden strong wind; brief storm
night-rack – thick storm clouds

Activities

Speaking and listening In groups, discuss the answers to these questions, then share your ideas in a class discussion.

1. What scene is described in lines 1–4? Which words and phrases in lines 5–7 suggest that life is hard for the fishermen and their families?

2. What do the wives do while their husbands are out fishing? List the words and phrases in verse 2 which suggest that the sea is becoming rough and dangerous.

3. What scene is described in lines 15–18? Which details create a picture of grief?

4. Look at the last three lines of each verse. Which words and phrases are the same in each verse? Discuss the message that these lines keep repeating.

In your group, prepare a reading of the poem which brings out the sadness of the story. Experiment with different ways of reading the two parts of each verse: for example, try reading the last three lines of each verse with just one person speaking them and then with the whole group chanting them. When you are satisfied with your reading, either tape-record it or present it to the rest of the class.

Reading and writing Look again at each verse of the poem. Write one or two sentences in your own words to sum up what is described in each verse. Then draw a picture-strip telling the story of the three fishermen. Either use the sentences you have written as captions for the pictures or choose suitable lines from the poem to use as captions.

Sand-strewn Caverns

About the poet

Matthew Arnold was the son of Thomas Arnold, the famous headmaster of Rugby public school. Matthew Arnold was a scholar who wrote important books on literary criticism, religion and education. From 1857 to 1867 he was Professor of Poetry at Oxford University.

About the poem

In these lines from a longer poem, 'The Forsaken Merman', based on a Danish legend, a woman remembers the caverns under the sea where she lived for a time with a merman.

ε Sand-strewn Caverns ε

Sand-strewn caverns, cool and deep,
Where the winds are all asleep;
Where the spent lights quiver and gleam,
Where the salt weed sways in the stream,
Where the sea-beasts, ranged all round,   5
Feed in the ooze of their pasture-ground;
Where the sea-snakes coil and twine,
Dry their mail and bask in the brine;
Where great whales come sailing by,
Sail and sail, with unshut eye,
Round the world for ever and aye ...

MATHEW ARNOLD
(1822–88)

ε ε

aye – ever

Activities

Speaking and listening

In pairs, discuss these questions, then share your ideas in a group or class discussion.

1. Talk about the first four lines. What picture do they give you of the caverns? List the words and phrases that give you that picture.

2. What do you learn about the sea-creatures which live around the caverns (lines 5–11)? List the words which describe how they behave. What does their behaviour tell you about what the caverns are like?

3. Talk about these words and decide which one sums up the mood of the poem:

   - sad
   - wistful
   - gloomy
   - solemn
   - cheerful.

Creative writing

Imagine you have been asked to paint a picture or to compose a piece of music to capture the mood of the poem. Either

- describe the type of painting you would try to produce. For example, how dark/light would it be? Would the colours be soft/bright/dull? What would be the main colours you would use?

or

- describe the type of music you would try to compose. Which type of instruments would the music be for? Would the piece be fast or slow? Would it be mainly loud or soft?

Work together and use a synthesiser to compose a piece of music or work on your own and either do a painting or use computer graphics to create an illustrated version of the poem.

Break, break, break

About the poet

For details of Alfred, Lord Tennyson see page 1.

About the poem

In these lines, written shortly after the death of one of Tennyson's friends, the poet expresses his grief.

Break, break, break

Break, break, break,
    On thy cold gray stones, O Sea!
And I would that my tongue could utter
    The thoughts that arise in me.

O well for the fisherman's boy   5
    That he shouts with his sister at play!
O well for the sailor lad,
    That he sings in his boat on the bay!

And the stately ships go on
    To their haven under the hill;   10
But O for the touch of a vanish'd hand,
    And the sound of a voice that is still!

Break, break, break,
    At the foot of thy crags, O Sea!
But the tender grace of a day that is dead   15
    Will never come back to me.

ALFRED, LORD TENNYSON
(1809–92)

Activities

Speaking and listening

Discuss these questions in groups. Choose someone to act as secretary to keep notes of your ideas, then share them in a class discussion.

1. Discuss how the mood of the poem is set in the first verse. What does the phrase 'cold gray stones' suggest? What do you learn about how much his grief is affecting Tennyson from lines 3 and 4?

2. Talk about the people Tennyson describes in the second verse. Who are they? What are they doing? How do their moods and behaviour *contrast* with Tennyson's?

3. How do the first two lines in verse 3 provide a contrast with the last two lines of the verse? What does 'haven' suggest about the ships' journeys? What do 'vanish'd hand' and 'a voice that is still' tell you about his friend's journey?

4. How are the first two lines of verse 4 similar to the first two lines of verse 1? What does this suggest? Discuss how Tennyson uses the image of the sea continuing to break against the crags to provide a *contrast* with his own loss.

5. Which of the verses do you think expresses Tennyson's grief most effectively? Give reasons for your answer.

In pairs, prepare a reading of the poem to portray to your listeners just how much Tennyson misses his dead friend. Think carefully about which words you need to *stress* and what the *pace* of your reading should be. Experiment with using two voices to read some lines and a single voice for others. Then take it in turns to present your readings to the rest of the class.

❧ Mystery and magic ❧

Lord Randal

About the poet

The author and date of this poem are unknown.

About the poem

This poem is a traditional ballad, which was spoken or sung by entertainers called minstrels, who travelled round the country during the Middle Ages. A **ballad** is a poem which is divided into short verses, and which tells a story. The verses usually have four lines and there may be a chorus that is repeated after each verse. In this ballad, there are two people speaking. The first two lines of each verse are spoken by the mother and the third and fourth lines are spoken by Lord Randal.

There are several versions of the poem from different parts of the country. This *dialect* version contains a number of words which are different from the words we use in standard English. For example, 'ye' is used for 'you', 'hae' for 'have', 'wald' for 'would' and 'gat' for 'got'.

❧ Lord Randal ❧

'O where hae ye been, Lord Randal, my son?
O where hae ye been, my handsome young man?'
'I hae been to the wild wood; mother, make my bed soon,
For I'm weary wi' hunting, and fain wald lie down.'

'Where gat ye your dinner, Lord Randal, my son?   5
Where gat ye your dinner, my handsome young man?'
'I dined wi' my true-love; mother, make my bed soon,
For I'm weary wi' hunting, and fain wald lie down.'

'What gat ye to your dinner, Lord Randal, my son?
What gat ye to your dinner, my handsome young man?'   10
'I gat eels boiled in broo'; mother, make my bed soon,
For I'm weary wi' hunting, and fain wald lie down.'

'What became of your bloodhounds, Lord Randal, my son?
What became of your bloodhounds, my handsome young man?'
'O they swelled and they died; mother, make my bed soon,   15
For I'm weary wi' hunting, and fain wald lie down.'

'O I fear ye are poisoned, Lord Randal, my son!
O I fear ye are poisoned, my handsome young man!'
'O yes! I am poisoned; mother, make my bed soon,
For I'm weary wi' hunting, and fain wald lie down.'   20

Anon

fain – gladly
broo' – broth

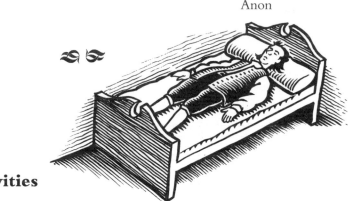

Activities

Reading and writing   Read the poem, then write answers to these questions.

1. Where has Lord Randal been and what has happened to him?

2. Do you think what happened was an accident or murder? Say why.

3. What kind of story is the story of Lord Randal? Is it:

   - a story of treachery
   - a story of foolishness
   - a story of enchantment
   - a tragic story
   - a romantic story
   - a story of revenge?

   Give reasons for your answer.

Speaking and listening   In pairs, role-play a scene in which Lord Randal's mother explains to a friend what happened to her son.

This is a poem in which rhythm and repetition are used to build up towards a dramatic ending in the final verse. In pairs, prepare a presentation of the ballad. Try to vary the *pace* and the volume to show the mother's increasing anxiety and distress as her son finally admits what has happened to him.

The Listeners

About the poet

Walter de la Mare was a poet and novelist. His first book was published under the name of Walter Ramal, which is part of his surname read in a mirror. Poems from his verses for children, *Peacock Pie* (1913), have remained popular and can be found in many collections of poems.

About the poem

This is a **narrative poem**, a poem which tells a story. It tells the story of an incident on a moonlit night. The poet uses the rhythm to add to the atmosphere of mystery and suspense created by the words.

☙ The Listeners ☙

'Is there anybody there?' said the Traveller,
    Knocking on the moonlit door;
And his horse in the silence champed the grasses
    Of the forest's ferny floor:
And a bird flew up out of the turret,   5
    Above the Traveller's head:
And he smote upon the door again a second time;
    'Is there anybody there?' he said.
But no one descended to the Traveller;
    No head from the leaf-fringed sill   10
Leaned over and looked into his grey eyes,
    Where he stood perplexed and still.
But only a host of phantom listeners
    That dwelt in the lone house then

Stood listening in the quiet of the moonlight   15
    To that voice from the world of men:
Stood thronging the faint moonbeams on the dark stair,
    That goes down to the empty hall,
Hearkening in an air stirred and shaken
    By the lonely Traveller's call.   20
And he felt in his heart their strangeness,
    Their stillness answering his cry,
While his horse moved, cropping the dark turf,
    'Neath the starred and leafy sky;
For he suddenly smote on the door, even   25
    Louder, and lifted his head:-
'Tell them I came, and no one answered,
    That I kept my word,' he said.
Never the least stir made the listeners,
    Though every word he spake   30
Fell echoing through the shadowiness of the still house
    From the one man left awake:
Ay, they heard his foot upon the stirrup,
    And the sound of iron on stone,
And how the silence surged softly backward,   35
    When the plunging hoofs were gone.

WALTER DE LA MARE
(1873–1956)

turret – small tower
smote – struck
Hearkening – listening to

Activities

Speaking and listening In groups, discuss questions 1 to 3. Make notes of your answers, then share your views in a whole class discussion.

1. • Who do you think the traveller is?
   • Why do you think he has come to the house?
   • What sort of house do you think it is?
   • Who or what are the listeners?
   • How long ago do you think this incident happened?

2. The poem can be divided into four sections. Talk about what happens in the poem and decide where one section ends and the next begins.

3. List the words in the poem which describe sounds. In which sections of the poem are there noises? In which sections of the poem is there silence?

In groups of four, prepare a reading of the poem in order to create an atmosphere of mystery and suspense and to bring out its rhythm. You will need to think carefully about which *syllables* to *stress* in each line. Prepare for your reading by taking one of the sections and marking the three or four syllables in each line which are stressed. Here are the first two lines:

'Is there <u>any</u>body <u>there</u>?' said the <u>Trav</u>eller,
<u>Knock</u>ing on the <u>moonlit</u> <u>door</u>.

Take it in turns to present your readings to the rest of the class. Then, as a class, discuss which reading worked best and why.

Reading and writing

Here are some other possible titles for the poem:

- The enchanted house
- The promise
- The traveller's return
- The midnight call.

Which of these other titles do you prefer? Give your reasons. Do you think 'The Listeners' is the best title for the poem? Give reasons for your answer.

La Belle Dame sans Merci

About the poet

John Keats trained as a medical student. One of his fellow students described him as an idle loafing fellow, always writing poetry. He quickly established a reputation as one of the leading poets of the time, but died when he was only 25. His famous poems include the 'Ode to Autumn'. Another of his poems, 'On the Sea', can be found on page 24.

About the poem

This poem is a **ballad** (see p. 29) which tells the story of a knight who has fallen in love with an enchantress. In the poem, there are two voices: in the first three verses, someone asks the knight what is wrong; in the remainder of the poem, the knight explains the reasons why he is so distressed. The title of the poem, 'La Belle Dame sans Merci', means 'The beautiful lady without pity'.

◄ *La Belle Dame sans Merci* ◄

'O what can ail thee, knight-at-arms,
    Alone and palely loitering?
The sedge has withered from the lake,
    And no birds sing.

'O what can ail thee, knight-at-arms,   5
    So haggard and so woe-begone?
The squirrel's granary is full,
    And the harvest's done.

'I see a lily on thy brow
    With anguish moist and fever dew,   10
And on thy cheeks a fading rose
    Fast withereth too.'

I met a lady in the meads
    Full beautiful – a faery's child,
Her hair was long, her foot was light,   15
    And her eyes were wild.

I made a garland for her head,
    And bracelets too, and fragrant zone;
She look'd at me as she did love,
    And made sweet moan.   20

I set her on my pacing steed,
    And nothing else saw all day long,
For sidelong would she bend, and sing
    A faery's song.

She found me roots of relish sweet,   25
    And honey wild, and manna dew,
And sure in language strange she said –
    'I love thee true.'

She took me to her elfin grot,
    And there she wept, and sigh'd full sore,   30
And there I shut her wild, wild eyes
    With kisses four.

And there she lullēd me asleep,
  And there I dream'd – Ah! woe betide!
The latest dream I ever dreamed   35
  On the cold hill's side.

I saw pale kings, and princes too,
  Pale warriors, death-pale were they all;
They cried, 'La Belle Dame sans Merci
  Hath thee in thrall!'   40

I saw their starv'd lips in the gloam,
  With horrid warning gapēd wide,
And I awoke and found me here,
  On the cold hill's side.

And this is why I sojourn here,   45
  Alone and palely loitering,
Though the sedge is withered from the lake,
  And no birds sing.

JOHN KEATS
(1795–1821)

⇆ ⇆

ail – trouble
sedge – coarse grass/rushes
haggard – looking wild and worried
woe begone – sad and sorrowful
meads – meadows
steed – horse

manna – heavenly food
elfin grot – fairy's cave or grotto
in thrall – in captivity
gloam – twilight
sojourn – stay temporarily

Activities

Reading and writing

Read the poem, then write answers to these questions.

1. What do you learn about the knight from the first three verses? Which words and phrases tell you about

   ● his appearance
   ● his feelings?

2. How does the person who speaks the first three verses feel about the knight? Does the speaker

   ● feel sorry for the knight

- not care about the knight
- feel curious about knight
- feel anxious about the knight
- feel sympathy for the knight?

Give reasons for your answer.

3. What attracted the knight to the lady? How can you tell from her appearance and her behaviour towards him that she is an enchantress?

4. ● Why did the knight fall asleep?
   - Who did he see in his dream?
   - Why does he say their lips are 'starv'd'?
   - What is their 'horrid warning'?

5. Notice how the last verse is similar to the first verse. List the words and phrases which Keats repeats in order to stress the knight's situation.

Speaking and listening   Imagine you are a storyteller who has heard the story of 'La Belle Dame sans Merci'. Retell the story as you might tell it to a group of listeners. Keep to the main outline of the story and its medieval setting, but adapt or add any details that you want to and use any of Keats' words and phrases that fit your way of telling the tale.

A Lyke-wake Dirge

About the poet

The author and date of this poem are unknown.

About the poem

The poem is in the form of a dirge or chant made by mourners, who are attending a wake, during which they keep watch over a dead body the night before the funeral. The mourners are thinking of the fate of the person's spirit, as it makes its final journey.

The poem is written in a *dialect*, which is different in a number of ways from modern standard English. For example, at the time it was written it was common in many dialects to use 'thou', 'thee' and 'thy' instead of 'you' and 'your'. The poem also contains a number of dialect words, such as 'ae' meaning 'one' and 'Whinny-muir' which means a moor (muir) covered in gorse (whinny). In addition, some words in the poem are not spelt in the usual way. For example, 'none' is spelt 'nane' and 'bone' is spelt 'bane'. They are spelt in this way because this is how they were pronounced.

⮌ *A Lyke-wake Dirge* ⮌

This ae nighte, this ae nighte,
   – Every nighte and alle,
Fire and fleet and candle-lighte,
   And Christe receive thy saule.

When thou from hence away art past,   5
   – Every nighte and alle,
To Whinny-muir thou com'st at last;
   And Christe receive thy saule.

If ever thou gavest hosen and shoon,
   – Every nighte and alle,   10
Sit thee down and put them on;
   And Christe receive thy saule.

If hosen and shoon thou ne'er gav'st nane
   – Every nighte and alle,
The whinnes sall prick thee to the bare bane;   15
   And Christe receive thy saule.

From Whinny-muir when thou mayst pass,
   – Every nighte and alle,
To Brig o' Dread thou com'st at last;
   And Christe receive thy saule.   20

From Brig o' Dread when thou mayst pass,
   – Every nighte and alle,
To Purgatory fire thou com'st at last;
   And Christe receive thy saule.

If ever thou gavest meat or drink,   25
   – Every nighte and alle,
The fire sall never make thee shrink;
   And Christe receive thy saule.

If meat or drink thou ne'er gav'st nane,
   – Every nighte and alle,   30
The fire will burn thee to the bare bane;
   And Christe receive thy saule.

This ae nighte, this ae nighte,
  – *Every nighte and alle,*
Fire and fleet and candle-lighte,   35
  And Christe receive thy saule.

ANON

lyke-wyke – night watch (wake) over a dead body (lyke)
fleet – room in which corpse is laid
hosen and shoon – stockings and shoes
Brig o' Dread – Bridge of Dead across which dead souls have to pass
Purgatory fire – place of suffering where souls are cleansed of sin by fire

Activities

Speaking and listening

In groups discuss these questions. Make notes of your ideas, then share them in a class discussion.

1. Discuss how the mourners think that the way in which the person behaved in their life will decide what happens to them on their final journey. Look at verses 3 and 4. How might the dead person suffer when crossing Whinny-muir? How might their behaviour while alive protect them from suffering now that they are dead?

2. Look at verses 7 and 8. How might the dead person suffer in Purgatory? How might their behaviour while alive protect them from suffering now that they are dead?

3. Discuss what the *moral* of the dirge is.

This poem is a chant, which uses rhythm, rhyme and repetition to build up its effect. Choose one person to act as the 'chief mourner' and to lead the chant by reading the first and third lines of each verse, while the rest of the group acts as a chorus chanting the second and fourth lines, which are repeated as a *refrain* throughout the whole poem. Imagine you are mourners and practise chanting it in the way a group of mourners would chant it. Before you begin, decide what impression you want your chanting to create. You could add to your performance either by choosing some suitable background music to accompany it or by making masks to wear or hold in front of your faces. If you can perform it in a drama studio, you could also use lighting effects to create a suitable atmosphere.

Kubla Khan

About the poet

Coleridge was a close friend of William Wordsworth (see p. 80). His most famous poem is 'The Rime of the Ancient Mariner'. In the later years of his life he became addicted to opium, which he started to take in order to relieve the pain of rheumatism.

About the poem

Coleridge says that the poem came to him in a dream. He fell asleep while reading about the palace of Kubla Khan, the Mongol Emperor who ruled China during the thirteenth century. As soon as he awoke, he started to write the poem. But someone arrived to see him on business and he was interrupted. When he went back to finish the poem, he was unable to remember the rest of the dream.

The poem itself is like a dream and each of the sections is almost like a separate poem.

☙ Kubla Khan ☙

In Xanadu did Kubla Khan
A stately pleasure-dome decree:
Where Alph, the sacred river, ran
Through caverns measureless to man
   Down to a sunless sea.
So twice five miles of fertile ground   5
With walls and towers were girdled round:
And there were gardens bright with sinuous rills,
Where blossomed many an incense-bearing tree;
And here were forests ancient as the hills,   10
Enfolding sunny spots of greenery.

But oh! that deep romantic chasm which slanted
Down the green hill athwart a cedarn cover!
A savage place! as holy and enchanted
As e'er beneath a waning moon was haunted   15
By woman wailing for her demon-lover!
And from this chasm, with ceaseless turmoil seething,
As if this earth in fast thick pants were breathing,
A mighty fountain momently was forced:
Amid whose swift half-intermitted burst   20
Huge fragments vaulted like rebounding hail,
Or chaffy grain beneath the thresher's flail:
And 'mid these dancing rocks at once and ever
It flung up momently the sacred river.
Five miles meandering with a mazy motion   25
Through wood and dale the sacred river ran,
Then reached the caverns measureless to man,
And sank in tumult to a lifeless ocean:
And 'mid this tumult Kubla heard from far
Ancestral voices prophesying war!   30

    The shadow of the dome of pleasure
    Floated midway on the waves;
    Where was heard the mingled measure
    From the fountain and the caves.
It was a miracle of rare device,   35
A sunny pleasure-dome with caves of ice!

A damsel with a dulcimer
In a vision once I saw:
It was an Abyssinian maid,
And on her dulcimer she played,   40
Singing of Mount Abora.
Could I revive within me
Her symphony and song,
To such a deep delight 'twould win me
That with music loud and long   45
I would build that dome in air,
That sunny dome! those caves of ice!
And all who heard should see them there,
And all should cry, Beware! Beware!
His flashing eyes, his floating hair!   50
Weave a circle round him thrice,
And close your eyes with holy dread,
For he on honey-dew hath fed,
And drunk the milk of Paradise.

SAMUEL TAYLOR COLERIDGE
(1772–1834)

⋐ ⋑

sinuous rills – twisting streams   *momently* – for a moment
athwart – across   *dulcimer* – stringed instrument, plucked
cedarn – covering of cedar trees   like a harp

Activities

Reading and   In small groups, discuss these questions, then write answers
writing   to them.

Section 1

1. What is the 'stately pleasure-dome' (line 2) that Kubla
   Khan wanted?

2. In what kind of place did he order it to be made (lines
   3–5)?

3. What impression do you get of his pleasure-dome from
   lines 6–11? Pick out the words and phrases which give
   you that impression.

Section 2

4. What impression do you get of the pleasure-dome in this section? Which words and phrases tell us that it is a land of enchantment?

5. Which words and phrases in this section suggest violent movement and forces which Kubla Khan will be unable to control?

Section 3

6. What do the words 'shadow' (line 31) and 'miracle' (line 35) suggest about the pleasure-dome?

7. What impression of the pleasure-dome is given by line 36?

Section 4

8. Notice how in this section the poet is writing about himself rather than Kubla Khan. What is the vision that he recalls in lines 37–41?

9. Why does he wish he could remember 'her symphony and song' (line 42)? What does he say it would enable him to do (line 46)?

10. How does he think people would treat him if this happened? Pick out the words and phrases Coleridge uses in lines 50–4 to suggest that they would think he was under a spell.

Speaking and listening   Imagine you have been asked to prepare a radio broadcast of the poem. The producer proposes to use some music both before and after the reading to help capture the mood of the poem. What type of music would you choose? Can you suggest any particular pieces that you might use? Produce a group reading of the poem, if possible with a musical introduction and ending.

Ozymandias

About the poet

For details of Shelley see page 72.

About the poem

This poem is based on a story Shelley had read about a funeral temple of the Egyptian pharaoh, Rameses II, whom the Greeks called Ozymandias. According to the story, the temple bore an inscription which read: 'I am Ozymandias, king of kings; if anyone wishes to know how great I am and the place where kings like me lie, let him surpass any of my works'. Shelley knew that near the ruins of the temple were the shattered remains of an enormous statue of a pharaoh.

The poem is a **sonnet** (see p. 24) with an unusual **rhyme scheme** (see p. 19).

🐦 *Ozymandias* 🐦

I met a traveller from an antique land
Who said: 'Two vast and trunkless legs of stone
Stand in the desert… Near them, on the sand,
Half sunk, a shattered visage lies, whose frown,
And wrinkled lip, and sneer of cold command,   5
Tell that its sculptor well those passions read
Which yet survive, stamped on these lifeless things,
The hand that mocked them, and the heart that fed.
And on the pedestal these words appear:
"My name is Ozymandias, King of Kings: 10
Look on my works, ye Mighty, and despair!"
Nothing beside remains. Round the decay
Of that colossal wreck, boundless and bare,
The lone and level sands stretch far away.'

Percy Bysshe Shelley
(1792–1822)

🐦🐦

visage – face

Activities

Reading and writing

In pairs, read the poem and discuss these questions, then write answers to them.

1. Notice how the first line of the poem introduces the story as a traveller's tale. What does the traveller say he saw lying in the desert? Make a list of all the things he saw.

2. Which words tell you that it was once a very large statue? Why is the size of the statue important?

3. What did the sculptor who carved the statue think of Ozymandias? Which words in lines 4 and 5 tell you what the sculptor thought of the king?

4. What does the inscription tell you about Ozymandias and why he had the statue made?

5. What do the final three lines tell you about the statue and the place where it is lying? What do these lines tell you about history's view of Ozymandias and his statue?

6. What is the *moral* of the poem?

Speaking and listening

In pairs, take it in turns to retell the story of Ozymandias and his statue in order to make clear the *moral* of the story. Before you begin, make a list of the main points that you will need to include and, if necessary, refer to the list as you are telling the story.

Eldorado

About the poet

Edgar Allan Poe is most famous for his tales of terror and mystery, such as *The Pit and the Pendulum.* He was also the author of the first detective story, *The Murder in the Rue Morgue,* published in 1841. He wrote poems in many different styles, ranging from love poems to poems about strange and supernatural events.

About the poem

This poem is a **parable** – a story or wise saying in which the events are used in order to make a religious or moral point. You can find examples of parables in the Bible because Jesus often used parables when he spoke to his disciples (Luke 18: 1–30; 19: 11–27; Matthew 13: 3–23).

This poem tells the story of a knight's search for Eldorado, a legendary land supposed to be full of riches and opportunity.

Eldorado

Gaily bedight,
A gallant knight,
In sunshine and in shadow,
Had journeyed long,
Singing a song,   5
In search of Eldorado.

But he grew old –
This knight so bold –
And o'er his heart a shadow
Fell as he found   10
No spot of ground
That looked like Eldorado.

And, as his strength
Failed him at length,
He met a pilgrim shadow: 15
'Shadow,' said he,
'Where can it be,
This land of Eldorado?'

'Over the Mountains
Of the Moon,   20
Down the Valley of the Shadow,
Ride, boldly ride,'
The shade replied,
'If you seek for Eldorado.'

EDGAR ALLAN POE
(1809–49)

bedight – dressed

Activities

Reading and writing In pairs, discuss these questions, then write answers to them.

1. How is the knight feeling in the first verse? Which words and phrases tell you how he is feeling?

2. How does the knight's mood change in the second verse? What causes his mood to change?

3. What is the 'pilgrim shadow' (line 15)? Can you suggest what the poet uses the shadow to represent?

4. In verse 4, what advice does the pilgrim shadow give the knight? What do 'the Mountains of the Moon' and 'the Valley of Shadow' represent?

5. What is the meaning of this parable?

Speaking and listening Another poem which is a parable is 'Upon the Snail' (p. 18). In pairs, prepare readings of 'Eldorado' and 'Upon the Snail'. Write a short script to introduce your readings, in which you explain what a parable is and say what the message of each poem is. How does a parable differ from a **fable** (see p. 19)?

The Deserted House

About the poet

Mary Coleridge's great-grandfather was the brother of Samuel Taylor Coleridge (see p. 49). She was a novelist as well as a poet. Her books included *The King with Two Faces*, which is a historical story about the Swedish king Gustavus III.

About the poem

This poem consists of two six-line verses. Each verse uses a single rhyme at the end of the second, fourth and sixth lines.

≈ *The Deserted House* ≈

There's no smoke in the chimney,
  And the rain beats on the floor;
There's no glass in the window,
  There's no wood in the door;
The heather grows behind the house,
  And the sand lies before.

No hand hath trained the ivy,
  The walls are gray and bare,
The boats upon the sea sail by,
  Nor ever tarry there;
No beast of the field comes nigh,
  Nor any bird of the air.

MARY COLERIDGE
(1861–1907)

❧ ❧

tarry – wait or stay

Activities

Speaking and listening

In pairs, discuss these questions. Keep notes of your ideas, then share them in a group or class discussion.

1. Discuss what you learn from the first four lines about the appearance of the house.

2. What do you learn about where the house is situated from lines 5 and 6? Is it
   - on a moor
   - in a wood
   - by the sea
   - on a cliff?

3. In verse 2, what tells you that a) people and b) animals keep away from the house? What does this suggest about the house?

4. How does the poem make you feel about the house? Pick out the lines from the poem which give you that feeling.

5. Discuss who might have lived in the house and what might have happened there. Suggest some reasons why it is now deserted.

6. Talk about any deserted buildings that there are in your area or any ruins that you may have seen or visited while on holiday. Describe what they looked like and talk about why they have been deserted.

Creative writing

Either: Write a story which explains why the house is deserted. *Or:* Write a poem of your own about a deserted building (e.g., a deserted church, a deserted school or a deserted factory). Try to choose words and phrases that build up an air of mystery about the place in the way that Mary Coleridge does.

The Way through the Woods

About the poet

Kipling was born in India and worked there for a time as a journalist, after attending school in England. He is famous for his stories for children, such as the *Just-so Stories* and *The Jungle Book*. In 1907, he became the first British writer to be awarded the Nobel Prize for Literature.

About the poem

This poem does not follow any standard verse pattern. It achieves its effect through the poet's skilful use of rhythm, rhyme and repetition. In addition to rhymes at the end of lines, Kipling also makes use of a number of internal rhymes. An **internal rhyme** is a rhyme that is made between one of the words in a line and another word in the same line, usually the last word. For example, in line 3 of 'The way through the woods', 'rain' rhymes with 'again'. Try to spot more internal rhymes as you read through the poem.

❧ The Way through the Woods ☙

They shut the road through the woods
Seventy years ago.
Weather and rain have undone it again,
And now you would never know
There was once a road through the woods   5
Before they planted the trees.
It is underneath the coppice and heath
And the thin anemones.
Only the keeper sees
That, where the ring-dove broods,   10
And the badgers roll at ease,
There was once a road through the woods.

Yet, if you enter the woods
Of a summer evening late,
When the night-air cools on the trout-ringed pools   15
Where the otter whistles his mate,
(They fear not men in the woods,
Because they see so few.)
You will hear the beat of a horse's feet,
And the swish of a skirt in the dew,   20
Steadily cantering through
The misty solitudes,
As though they perfectly knew
The old lost road through the woods …
But there is no road through the woods.   25

RUDYARD KIPLING
(1865–1936)

❧ ❧

coppice – thicket of small trees

Activities

Reading and writing Read the poem, then discuss these questions in pairs before writing answers to them.

1. What does the first section (lines 1–5) tell you about the road through the woods?

2. What has happened to the wood since the road was closed? Pick out the details of plants and animals that are given in the second section (lines 6–12). Which words and phrases tell you how the wood has changed?

3. Who is 'the keeper' (line 9)? Why does Kipling stress that he is the only person who knows where the road used to be?

4. In the final section (lines 13–25), what sounds does Kipling describe? How do they help you to imagine the woods' past? How do they help to draw a contrast between the woods' present and the woods' past?

5. How would you describe the mood that the poem creates? Is it

- mysterious
- peaceful
- wistful
- menacing
- sad
- magical?

Give reasons for your answer.

6. Imagine that you visited the woods described in the poem one summer evening. Discuss what you would have seen and heard and how you would have felt, then write a diary entry describing your experience.

Speaking and listening

In groups, prepare a reading of the poem. What effect do you want your reading to have on your listeners? Experiment with different combinations of voices (e.g., individuals reading some lines, pairs or the whole group reading other lines) until you feel you are achieving the effect you want. Take it in turns to present your readings and discuss which reading worked best and why.

🕊 Weathers and seasons 🕊

Weathers

About the poet

Thomas Hardy is famous for his novels, such as *Tess of the D'Urbervilles* and *Far from the Madding Crowd*, set in the countryside around Dorset, which he called Wessex. Before becoming a writer, he trained as an architect. He published eight volumes of poetry.

About the poem

In this poem, Hardy writes about the weather at two different times of the year.

🕊 Weathers 🕊

I

This is the weather the cuckoo likes,
   And so do I;
When showers betumble the chestnut spikes,
   And nestlings fly:
And the little brown nightingale bills his best,   5
And they sit outside at 'The Travellers' Rest',
And maids come forth sprig-muslin drest,
And citizens dream of the south and west,
   And so do I.

II

This is the weather the shepherd shuns,   10
    And so do I;
When beeches drip in browns and duns,
    And thresh, and ply;
And hill-hid tides throb, throe on throe,
And meadow rivulets overflow,   15
And drops on gate-bars hang in a row,
And rooks in families homeward go,
    And so do I.

THOMAS HARDY
(1840–1928)

bills his best – sings loudest
sprig-muslin drest – wearing light cotton
    fabric with flower patterning
duns – dull brown

thresh – sway violently
ply – bend
tides – streams or rivers
throe on throe – rushing violently downstream

Activities

Reading and writing

Discuss these questions in pairs, then write answers to them.

1. Which details in verse 1 tell you what time of year it is and what the weather is like?

2. What tells you that birds and people like such weather?

3. Which details in verse 2 tell you what time of year it is and what the weather is like?

4. How do you know that birds and people don't like such weather?

Speaking and listening

Notice how Hardy repeats the phrase 'And so do I' to suggest that the person in the poem shares the same feelings about the weathers as other people. In pairs or groups prepare a reading of the poem in order to convey how people feel about the two different kinds of weathers.

Creative writing

Write a two-verse poem in which, like Thomas Hardy, you describe two contrasting types of weather. You could choose a place you know well and describe how different it is in different weathers. You could try to find photographs or do drawings to illustrate your poem.

Song: On May Morning

About the poet

John Milton was a poet and a political writer. During the English Civil War (1642–9) he wrote many political pamphlets supporting Parliament against the king. He is most famous for the long epic poem *Paradise Lost*, which he wrote after he had become totally blind.

About the poem

In this poem, Milton welcomes the arrival of May. The poem is divided into three parts. The first part gives a description of May's arrival, the second part is the song and the third part is like a formal greeting.

 Song: On May Morning

Now the bright morning star, Day's harbinger,
Comes dancing from the East, and leads with her
The flowery May, who from her green lap throws
The yellow cowslip, and the pale primrose.
    Hail, bounteous May! that dost inspire   5
    Mirth, and youth, and warm desire!
    Woods and groves are of thy dressing,
    Hill and dale doth boast thy blessing.
Thus we salute thee with our early song,
And welcome thee, and wish thee long.   10

JOHN MILTON
(1608–74)

harbinger – forerunner
bounteous – full of goodness
Mirth – laughter

Activities

Speaking and listening

In groups, discuss these questions. Keep notes of your ideas, then share them in a class discussion.

1. Discuss the picture of May's arrival given in lines 1–4. List the words and phrases which suggest that May's arrival is lively, bright and colourful.

2. In the song, why is the coming of May called 'a blessing'? What does it bring for people and nature?

3. Pick out the words and phrases in the final two lines which are used to make them sound like a formal greeting.

4. Milton presents both the sun and May as if they can behave like human beings. For example, in the first four lines he suggests that the sun is a person who comes dancing along, leading May by the hand and that May is scattering flowers from her lap. In the final two lines he greets May as if she is a newly arrived guest. Describing an animal, object or thing as though it is a person is called **personification**. Here are some more examples of personification:

   - Angrily the wind snatched the branches from the trees and snapped them in his hands.
   - The fog wrapped the city in her dark embrace.
   - Then autumn came, whistling cheerfully, bearing his promised gifts.

   Try to make up some other examples of personification to describe one of the other seasons or a type of weather (e.g., snow, hail or thunder).

In groups, prepare a reading of the poem. Experiment with different combinations of voices for the three sections of the poem.

A Summer Evening

About the poet

For details of Percy Bysshe Shelley see page 72.

About the poem

In these lines, from a longer poem called 'Evening', Shelley describes a summer evening. Before reading the poem, remind yourself what **alliteration** is (see p. 2) and what a **metaphor** is (see p. 22).

A Summer Evening

The sun is set; the swallows are asleep;
   The bats are flitting fast in the gray air;
The slow soft toads out of damp corners creep,
   And evening's breath, wandering here and there
Over the quivering surface of the stream,   5
Wakes not one ripple from its summer dream.

There is no dew on the dry grass tonight,
   Nor damp within the shadow of the trees;
The wind is intermitting, dry, and light;
   And in the inconstant motion of the breeze   10
The dust and straws are driven up and down,
And whirled about the pavement of the town.

PERCY BYSSHE SHELLEY
(1792–1822)

Activities

Reading and writing   Read the poem, then write answers to these questions.

1. List the details of the summer evening that Shelley includes in verse 1.

2. What use does he make of alliteration to draw attention to the way the bats and the toads move?

3. What metaphor does he use to suggest that the stream is hardly moving (lines 3–6)?

4. In the second verse, which words and phrases does Shelley use to suggest that the evening is very dry?

5. Which words in lines 9–12 tell you about the wind and what it is doing?

6. What impression of the summer evening does the poem give? Is it

   - hot
   - dry
   - still
   - cool
   - dusty
   - quiet
   - windy?

   Give reasons for the words you choose.

   Write a similar poem about a summer afternoon. Decide what sort of impression you want to create, and choose details and images that will help you to give that impression.

Autumn

About the poet

Only six of Hulme's poems were published in his lifetime. In 1912, he published his *Complete Poetical Works* consisting of five poems, the longest of which has nine lines. He was killed in action during the First World War.

About the poem

In this poem Hulme writes about a person out walking on an autumn night. He uses both **metaphors** and **similes** (see pp. 12 and 22) to create a picture of an autumn night.

Autumn

A touch of cold in the Autumn night –
I walked abroad,
And saw the ruddy moon lean over a hedge
Like a red-faced farmer.
I did not stop to speak, but nodded,   5
And round about were the wistful stars
With white faces like town children.

THOMAS ERNEST HULME
(1886–1917)

abroad – out of doors
ruddy – red-coloured
wistful – sadly thoughtful

Activities

Speaking and listening

Discuss these questions in groups. Make notes of your answers and then share your ideas in a class discussion.

1. Discuss the impression that the poem gives of the autumn night. What sort of night is it? Is it

   - cool and bright
   - crisp and clear
   - sharp and bitter
   - calm and chilly
   - cold and dark?

   Give reasons for your answer.

2. Talk about how Hulme uses a metaphor (saw the ruddy moon lean over a hedge) in line 3 and a simile (like a red-faced farmer) in line 4 to describe the moon. What do they suggest about the position and appearance of the moon?

3. Do you think the person is walking quickly, slowly or at a moderate pace? Give reasons for your answer.

4. Talk about how Hulme uses another metaphor in lines 6 and 7 and another simile in line 7 to describe the stars. What does the word 'wistful' suggest? Discuss how the simile in line 7 provides a contrast with the simile in line 4.

5. Imagine that you had to choose a series of pictures to illustrate the poem. Discuss the five pictures you would choose to illustrate:

   ● line 1
   ● line 2
   ● lines 3 and 4
   ● line 5
   ● lines 6 and 7.

   Either get a group member to draw rough sketches of your ideas or draw up written instructions for an artist, explaining what you want them to put in each picture.

Creative writing   Write a short poem in which your aim is to create a picture of a night or a morning at a particular time of year. Decide what impression you want your picture to give and try to include at least one metaphor or simile to help you to create that impression.

Fall, leaves, fall

About the poet

Emily Brontë is most famous for her novel *Wuthering Heights*. She and her sisters, Charlotte and Anne, lived in the isolated village of Haworth in Yorkshire, where their father was the vicar. Many of Emily Brontë's poems first appeared in a joint volume of poetry, which the three sisters published under the pen-names of Currer, Acton and Ellis Bell. The book sold only two copies, but fortunately that did not discourage the sisters from continuing to write.

About the poem

This poem describes someone looking forward to the arrival of winter. It was written when Emily Brontë was a teenager and is in **rhyming couplets** (see p. 4).

Fall, leaves, fall

Fall, leaves, fall; die, flowers, away;
Lengthen night and shorten day;
Every leaf speaks bliss to me
Fluttering from the autumn tree.
I shall smile when wreaths of snow   5
Blossom where the rose should grow;
I shall sing when night's decay
Ushers in a drearier day.

EMILY BRONTË
(1818–48)

Activities

Speaking and listening

In pairs, discuss these questions. Make notes of your ideas, then share them in a class or group discussion.

1. Discuss what the person feels about autumn and the arrival of winter. List the words and phrases which tell you about the person's feelings.

2. Make a list of the words which describe winter and its effects. What impression do they give of winter? Discuss how the person's feelings provide a *contrast* with this view of winter.

3. Talk about the mood of the poem. What word(s) would you choose to describe the mood of the poem? Here are some suggestions:
   - magical
   - sinister
   - happy
   - mysterious
   - haunting.

   Can you suggest any others? Give reasons for your views.

Creative writing

Work with a partner. What signs tell you that winter is approaching? How do you feel about the coming of winter? Make a list of words and ideas that you associate with the coming of winter, then draft a short poem of your own about the arrival of winter.

The Fog

 The Fog

I saw the fog grow thick,
   Which soon made blind my ken;
It made tall men of boys,
   And giants of tall men.

It clutched my throat, I coughed;   5
   Nothing was in my head
Except two heavy eyes
   Like balls of burning lead.

And when it grew so black
   That I could know no place,   10
I lost all judgment then,
   Of distance and of space.

The street lamps, and the lights
   Upon the halted cars,
Could either be on earth   15
   Or be the heavenly stars.

A man passed by me close;
   I asked my way; he said,
'Come, follow me, my friend' –
   I followed where he led.   20

He rapped the stones in front,
  'Trust me,' he said, 'and come,'
I followed like a child –
  A blind man led me home.

W.H. DAVIES
(1871–1940)

ken – range of vision
rapped – tapped with a stick

Activities

Reading and writing

Read the poem and discuss these questions in pairs, then write answers to them.

1. As the fog develops, how does it start to affect the person's sight (lines 3 and 4)?

2. What does the word 'clutched' suggest (line 5)?

3. In verse 2, the poet uses a **simile** (see p. 12). Copy out the simile, and explain in your own words what it tells you about the effect of the fog.

4. What happens to the person when the fog thickens (lines 9–16)?

5. How do you think the person feels when someone offers to help him?

6. At which point does the person realise that the man helping him is blind?

7. How does the person feel as the blind man leads him home?

'The Fog' is written in four line verses, each of which has the same pattern of rhymes. Remind yourself what a **rhyme scheme** is (see p. 19), then work out the rhyme scheme of 'The Fog'.

Imagine you are standing on a cliff overlooking a busy harbour when a mist comes rolling in from the sea. Write a short poem describing how everything gradually disappears from your sight. Do not worry about trying to make it rhyme, unless you want to do so. If you decide you do want to make it rhyme, you could try to write four line verses using the rhyme scheme that W.H. Davies uses in 'The Fog'.

Winter

About the poet

Percy Bysshe Shelley was educated at Eton before going to Oxford University. However, his outspoken views led him to be expelled from Oxford. He married at the age of 20, but separated from his wife, who later committed suicide. Following her death, Shelley went to live in Italy. He was drowned at sea shortly before his thirtieth birthday. Other poems by Shelley can be found on pages 53 and 65.

About the poem

In these lines Shelley describes the strength and power of winter by writing as if winter is a person. Before reading the poem, remind yourself what **personification** is (see p. 64).

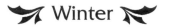 Winter

Winter came: the wind was his whip:
One choppy finger was on his lip;
He had torn the cataracts from the hills,
And they clanked at his girdle like manacles.
His breath was a chain which without a sound   5
The earth, and the air, and the water bound;
He came, fiercely driven in his chariot-throne
By the tenfold blasts of the arctic zone.
Then the weeds which were forms of living death
Fled from the frost to the earth beneath.   10
Their decay and sudden flight from frost
Was but like the vanishing of a ghost.

PERCY BYSSHE SHELLEY
(1792–1822)

choppy – craggy and gnarled
cataracts – waterfalls
girdle – belt
manacles – handcuffs

Activities

Speaking and listening

Discuss these questions in pairs, then share your ideas in a group or class discussion.

1. Talk about how Shelley suggests that winter is strong and powerful. Make a list of the words and phrases which suggest winter's strength and power.

2. What sort of person is winter compared with? What does this tell us about winter?

3. The poem is written in **rhyming couplets** (see p. 4). Which pair of lines do you think is the most effective? Give reasons for your view.

Creative writing

Write a poem about one of the other seasons, in which you describe it by *comparing* it with a person. Before you start, think carefully about what the season is like, then decide what sort of person you are going to compare the season with and what impression of the season you want your comparison to create.

When icicles hang by the wall

About the poet

William Shakespeare was born in Stratford-upon-Avon and became England's most famous playwright. His 37 plays include *Hamlet, Julius Caesar, Macbeth* and *Romeo and Juliet*.

About the poem

In some of his plays, Shakespeare included a number of songs. This song about winter is at the very end of the comedy *Love's Labours Lost*.

🖋 When icicles hang by the wall 🖋

When icicles hang by the wall,
   And Dick the shepherd blows his nail,
And Tom bears logs into the hall,
   And milk comes frozen home in pail;
When blood is nipp'd and ways be foul,   5
Then nightly sings the staring owl,
     Tu-whit! tu-who!
     A merry note,
While greasy Joan doth keel the pot.

When all aloud the wind doth blow,   10
   And coughing drowns the parson's saw,
And birds sit brooding in the snow,
   And Marian's nose looks red and raw;
When roasted crabs hiss in the bowl,
Then nightly sings the staring owl,   15
     Tu-whit! tu-who!
     A merry note,
While greasy Joan doth keel the pot.

WILLIAM SHAKESPEARE
(1564–1616)

🖋 🖋

nipp'd – made painful by cold
ways be foul – paths/roads are muddy
keel – cool by stirring
saw – sermon

Activities

Speaking and listening

Read the poem and make notes in answer to these two questions, then share your ideas in a group discussion.

1. List the details about
   - the world outside
   - the people

   that Shakespeare includes in lines 1–5 and 11–14 to suggest that it is very cold.

2. Which lines tell us that although it is cold outside, it is warm and cheerful inside?

Prepare a group reading of the poem. Experiment with a mixture of solo, pair and group voices to bring out the contrast between the cold scene outside and the warm scene inside.

Creative writing   Shakespeare was writing about winter 400 years ago. Make lists of details about outdoor scenes and indoor scenes that you would include in a description of winter today. Use your notes as the basis for writing either your own poem about winter or a short prose description of winter in which, like Shakespeare, you provide a contrast between the cold outside and the warmth inside. If you choose to write a poem, you could write a song, using the type of verse form that someone would use when writing a song for a modern musical.

Snow

About the poet

For details of Edward Thomas see page 15.

About the poem

This poem presents a young child's view of what has caused the snow and her feelings about it.

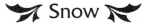 Snow

In the gloom of whiteness,
In the great silence of snow,
A child was sighing
And bitterly saying: 'Oh,
They have killed a white bird up there on her nest,   5
The down is fluttering from her breast.'
And still it fell through that dusky brightness
On the child crying for the bird of the snow.

EDWARD THOMAS
(1878–1917)

Activities

Speaking and listening

In pairs, discuss these questions. Make notes of your answers, then share your ideas in either a class or group discussion.

1. What does the child feel about the snow? Make a list of the words which tell you how she feels.

2. What does the child think is causing the snow?

3. What picture is created by the last two lines?

4. 'Snow' was written in January 1915. Thomas wrote two drafts of the poem before he was satisfied with it. A **draft** is an unfinished piece of writing, which the writer keeps changing as he or she searches for words and phrases to express their ideas. Below are the two drafts of 'Snow'. *Compare* them with the finished poem. Discuss the main changes that Thomas made and suggest why he made them.

Snow: first draft

In the gloom of whiteness,
In the great silence of snow
A   sigh
~~The~~ child was ~~cry~~ing
     bitterly saying
And ~~saying bitterly~~: '~~You know~~, 'Oh,
They have killed a white bird up there on her nest,
~~And~~ The feathers are fluttering down from her breast.'
       ~~fell through~~
~~And still the snow was falling in that dusky brightness,~~
~~The child was crying for the snow, the snow,~~
They were
~~It was~~ falling still through that dusky brightness
          ~~at the bird of the snow~~.
And the child was crying ~~for the bird of the snow.~~
         for the snow, the snow.
         for the dying of the snow.

Snow: second draft

In the gloom of the whiteness,
In the great silence of snow,
A child was sighing
And bitterly saying, 'Oh
They have killed a white bird up there on her nest,
    down is
The ~~feathers are~~ fluttering from her breast.'
And still it fell
~~They were falling still~~ through that dusky brightness
On
~~And~~ the child ~~was~~ crying for the bird of snow.

London Snow

About the poet

Robert Bridges was educated at Eton and Oxford University, where he rowed for his college. He worked as a doctor, before becoming a full-time writer. From 1913 to 1930 he was Poet Laureate.

About the poem

In this poem Bridges describes a heavy overnight snowfall and how the people in the city react to it.

London Snow

When men were all asleep the snow came flying,
In large white flakes falling on the city brown,
Stealthily and perpetually settling and loosely lying,
    Hushing the latest traffic of the drowsy town;
Deadening, muffling, stifling its murmurs failing;   5
Lazily and incessantly floating down and down:
    Silently sifting and veiling road, roof and railing;
Hiding difference, making unevenness even,
Into angles and crevices softly drifting and sailing.
    All night it fell, and when full inches seven   10

It lay in the depth of its uncompacted lightness,
The clouds blew off from a high and frosty heaven;
   And all woke earlier for the unaccustomed brightness
Of the winter dawning, the strange unheavenly glare:
The eye marvelled – marvelled at the dazzling whiteness;   15
   The ear hearkened to the stillness of the solemn air;
No sound of wheel rumbling nor of foot falling,
And the busy morning cries came thin and spare.
   Then boys I heard, as they went to school, calling;
They gathered up the crystal manna to freeze   20
Their tongues with tasting, their hands with snowballing;
   Or rioted in a drift, plunging up to the knees;
Or peering up from under the white-mossed wonder,
'O look at the trees!' they cried, 'O look at the trees!'
   With lessened load a few carts creak and blunder,   25
Following along the white deserted way,
A country company long dispersed asunder:
   When now already the sun, in pale display
Standing by Paul's high dome, spread forth below
His sparkling beams, and awoke the stir of the day.   30
   For now doors open, and war is waged with the snow;
And trains of sombre men, past tale of number,
Tread long brown paths, as toward their toil they go:
   But even for them awhile no cares encumber
Their minds diverted; the daily word is unspoken,   35
The daily thoughts of labour and sorrow slumber
At the sight of the beauty that greets them, for the charm
     they have broken.

ROBERT BRIDGES
(1844–1930)

manna – heavenly food
dispersed asunder – scattered in all directions
dome – St Paul's Cathedral
encumber – burden

Activities

Reading and writing

Discuss these questions in pairs and then write answers to them.

1. Look at the description of the snow falling (lines 1–9). Make lists of the words Bridges uses to describe the snow falling. What do these words suggest about how the snow falls?

2. How is the city changed by the snowfall? Which lines tell you how the city has changed?

3. How do people react when they wake up and see the change?

4. What do the children do on their way to school? How does Bridges show that they are

   - amazed
   - excited by the snow?

5. Which words and phrases in lines 25–8 suggest that the snow has made travelling difficult?

6. What picture is created by the phrase 'war is waged with the snow' (line 31)?

7. What impression of the people going to work does Bridges create in lines 32–3? How is their mood different because of the snow (lines 34–7)?

In the poem, Bridges uses lines of different length and varies the number of *stressed* and *unstressed* syllables to help change the *pace* and rhythm of the poem. For example, the first three lines all have a different number of syllables. This helps to suggest the way the snow is falling. In groups, work out a reading of the poem. You will need to decide which lines need only one speaker and which need several speakers.

Skating at Night

Skating at Night

And in the frosty season, when the sun
Was set, and visible for many a mile
The cottage windows through the twilight blaz'd,
I heeded not the summons. Clear and loud
The village clock tolled six; I wheeled about   5
Proud and exulting, like an untired horse,
That cares not for his home. All shod with steel,
We hissed along the polished ice in games
Confederate, imitative of the chase
And woodland pleasures, the resounding horn,   10
The pack loud bellowing, and the hunted hare.
So through the darkness and the cold we flew,
And not a voice was idle. With the din,
Meanwhile, the precipices rang aloud;
The leafless trees and every icy crag   15
Tinkled like iron; while the distant hills
Into the tumult sent an alien sound

Of melancholy, not unnoticed; while the stars,
Eastward, were sparkling clear, and in the west
The orange sky of evening died away.   20

WILLIAM WORDSWORTH
(1770–1850)

heeded – paid attention to
shod – wearing skates
Confederate – playing together like conspirators

Activities

Reading and writing

Read the poem, then discuss these questions in pairs and write answers to them. Before you begin, remind yourselves what **alliteration** is (see p. 2) and what a **simile** is (see p. 12).

1. In lines 1–3 which words and phrases suggest darkness and cold?

2. What is 'the summons' (line 4)? Why doesn't he respond to it and how does he feel about not doing so?

3. Once he has decided to ignore the summons, how do his feelings change (lines 5–7)? What simile does Wordsworth use to tell us how his feelings have changed?

4. How does Wordsworth use alliteration in lines 7 and 8 to suggest the sound and movement of skaters?

5. How does Wordsworth tell us that the games they played were noisy and vigorous (lines 8–13)?

6. Pick out the words and phrases that Wordsworth uses to describe the echo of their shouts (lines 13–18)? Why is the distant echo 'an alien sound of melancholy'? What does it remind Wordsworth that he should have done?

7. How does Wordsworth contrast the appearance of the stars and the setting of the sun in lines 19 and 20?

Write a poem based on a memory; for example, of a time when you stayed out late to finish a game you were playing, or of taking part in a games lesson or going for a cross-country run on a cold winter's day. Try to describe the scene as well as your feelings. You could try writing your poem in blank verse.

People and places

The Miller

About the poet

Geoffrey Chaucer was the greatest English poet of the Middle Ages. He came from a middle-class family and worked as a government official. His most famous work is *The Canterbury Tales*, which is a collection of stories told by a party of pilgrims on a journey from London to Canterbury to visit the shrine of Thomas à Becket.

About the poem

The description of 'The Miller' comes from the Introduction to *The Canterbury Tales*, known as 'The Prologue', in which Chaucer gives a pen-portrait of each of the pilgrims. Chaucer wrote in a *dialect* of Middle English, used by people from about 1100 to 1485, from which standard English later developed. The meanings of some words have changed completely since Chaucer used them, while others have dropped out of the language altogether. The modern translation of the description of the miller is by Nevill Coghill.

The Miller

The Millere was a stout carl for the nones;
Ful byg he was of brawn, and eek of bones.
That proved wel, for over al ther he cam,
At wrastlynge he wolde have alwey the ram.
He was short-sholdred, brood, a thikke knarre;   5
Ther was no dore that he nolde heve of harre,
Or breke it at a rennyng with his heed.
His berd as any sowe or fox was reed,
And therto brood, as though it were a spade.
Upon the cop right of his nose he hade   10
A werte, and theron stood a toft of herys,
Reed as the brustles of a sowes erys;

His nosethirles blake were and wyde.
A swerd and bokeler bar he by his syde.
His mouth as greet was as a greet forneys. 15
He was a janglere and a goliardeys,
And that was moost of synne and harlotries.
Wel koude he stelen corn and tollen thries;
And yet he hadde a thombe of gold, pardee.
A whit cote and a blew hood wered he. 20
A baggepipe wel koude he blowe and sowne,
And therwithal he broghte us out of towne.

GEOFFREY CHAUCER
(1340?–1400)

The Miller was a chap of sixteen stone,
A great stout fellow big in brawn and bone.
He did well out of them, for he could go
And win the ram at any wrestling show.
Broad, knotty and short-shouldered, he would boast 5
He could heave any door off hinge and post,
Or take a run and break it with his head.
His beard, like any sow or fox, was red
And broad as well, as though it were a spade;
And, at its very tip, his nose displayed 10
A wart on which there stood a tuft of hair
Red as the bristles in an old sow's ear.
His nostrils were as black as they were wide,
He had a sword and buckler at his side,
His mighty mouth was like a furnace door. 15
A wrangler and buffoon, he had a store
Of tavern stories, filthy in the main.
His was a master-hand at stealing grain.
He felt it with his thumb and thus he knew
Its quality and took three times his due – 20
A thumb of gold, by God, to gauge an oat!
He wore a hood of blue and a white coat.
He liked to play his bagpipes up and down
And that was how he brought us out of town.

Activities

(see p. 12)

Speaking and listening

In pairs, read Chaucer's description of 'The Miller', then use Nevill Coghill's translation of it to help you to understand the words and phrases in Chaucer's language which are different from standard English.

In groups, study Chaucer's original text and discuss these questions. Keep notes of your ideas, then share them in a class discussion.

1. Talk about the words and phrases that Chaucer uses to describe the miller's appearance. Make a list of them and discuss what you learn from the description about the miller's size and strength and his character.

2. Which of these words would you use to describe the miller:

   - aggressive
   - honest
   - dirty-minded
   - quarrelsome
   - devious
   - coarse?

   Can you suggest any others? Give reasons for your views.

3. Remind yourselves what a **simile** is (see p. 12), then pick out the similes that Chaucer uses in the description. Which of them do you think is most effective in developing the portrait?

4. Do you think Chaucer approves or disapproves of the miller? Which of these statements sums up Chaucer's attitude towards the miller:

   - a quarrelsome buffoon
   - a loudmouthed bully
   - a likeable rogue
   - an irritating, noisy companion?

   Give reasons for your views.

Creative writing

Work in a group. Use the library to find out which other characters Chaucer describes in *The Canterbury Tales*. Find out what their jobs were and what clothes they wore and make a wallchart about them.

Imagine you have been asked to write pen-portraits of a group of modern tourists waiting to board a bus or a plane. Write some lines describing one of them. Include details that describe their character as well as their appearance and make the portrait realistic, in the way the Chaucer gives us a realistic picture of the miller.

Work with a partner. Make a list of words that Chaucer uses in his text and use the translation to work out their meanings, then write some entries for a dictionary of Chaucer's language.

The Village Schoolmaster

About the poet

Oliver Goldsmith was born in Ireland and trained as a doctor, before becoming a writer. He is most famous for his play, *She Stoops to Conquer,* a comedy which is still very popular. Although he was a successful writer, Goldsmith was not good at looking after his money and was deep in debt when he died.

About the poem

The description of the village schoolmaster is taken from a long poem, 'The Deserted Village', which describes a country village as it was being destroyed by commercial developments. It is written in **rhyming couplets** (see p. 4).

 The Village Schoolmaster

Beside yon straggling fence that skirts the way,
With blossomed furze unprofitably gay,
There, in his noisy mansion, skilled to rule,
The village master taught his little school;
A man severe he was, and stern to view;   5
I knew him well, and every truant knew;
Well had the boding tremblers learned to trace
The day's disasters in his morning face;
Full well they laughed, with counterfeited glee,
At all his jokes, for many a joke had he;   10
Full well the busy whisper, circling round,
Conveyed the dismal tidings when he frowned;
Yet he was kind, or, if severe in aught,

The love he bore to learning was in fault;
The village all declared how much he knew;   15
'Twas certain he could write, and cypher too;
Lands he could measure, terms and tides presage,
And even the story ran that he could gauge.
In arguing too, the parson owned his skill,
For even tho' vanquished, he could argue still,   20
While words of learned length, and thundering sound,
Amazed the gazing rustics ranged around;
And still they gazed, and still the wonder grew,
That one small head could carry all he knew.

OLIVER GOLDSMITH
(1728–74)

furze – gorse
boding tremblers – pupils trembling
   with fear
counterfeited – pretended
aught – anything
cypher – do arithmetic

terms – days when quarterly accounts and
   wages were paid
tides – feast days
presage – predict
gauge – estimate the volume of barrels, etc.
vanquished – defeated

Activities

Speaking and listening   In groups, discuss these questions. Keep notes of your ideas, then share them in a class discussion.

1. Here are some statements about the schoolmaster. Say whether you agree or disagree with them and give reasons for your views:

   ● he was strict
   ● he was moody
   ● he often told jokes, which the children enjoyed
   ● he was a very learned man
   ● he could argue better than the parson
   ● the villagers admired him.

2. Discuss what the poet thinks of the schoolmaster. Does he

   ● admire him
   ● respect him
   ● disapprove of him?

   Give reasons for your view. Can you find any evidence to suggest that the poet is amused by the schoolmaster?

Creative writing
Goldsmith describes the schoolmaster's character rather than his appearance. Write a similar poem about someone you know well in which you describe their character rather than their appearance. Prepare for your writing by making notes listing the things you want your poem to say about the person's character, then decide whether you are going to write free verse or a rhyming poem. You could try writing it in couplets.

Elegy Written in a Country Churchyard

About the poet

Thomas Gray was one of the leading scholars of his time and spent most of his life living in Cambridge. His 'Elegy Written in a Country Churchyard' is one of the most well-known poems in the English language.

About the poem

An **elegy** is a poem written about someone who has died, in which the poet expresses his sorrow, love and respect for the dead person. In this poem, Gray remembers and praises all the ordinary people buried in the village graveyard, not just one famous person. These lines are from the opening of the poem, which was written about the churchyard at Stoke Poges in Buckinghamshire.

Elegy Written in a Country Churchyard

The curfew tolls the knell of parting day,
The lowing herd wind slowly o'er the lea,
The ploughman homeward plods his weary way,
And leaves the world to darkness and to me.

Now fades the glimmering landscape on the sight, 5
And all the air a solemn stillness holds,
Save where the beetle wheels his droning flight,
And drowsy tinklings lull the distant folds;

Save that from yonder ivy-mantled tow'r
The moping owl does to the moon complain   10
Of such as, wand'ring near her secret bow'r,
Molest her ancient solitary reign.

Beneath those rugged elms, that yew-tree's shade,
Where heaves the turf in many a mould'ring heap,
Each in his narrow cell for ever laid,   15
The rude forefathers of the hamlet sleep.

THOMAS GRAY
(1716–71)

Curfew – bell rung at the same time each evening
knell – sound (of funeral bell)
lea – grassland
save – except
wheels – flies in circular movements
drowsy tinklings – soft sound of bells hung around sheeps' necks
secret bow'r – hidden territory or nest
rude – uneducated

Activities

Speaking and listening In pairs, discuss these questions, then work together to produce a reading of the poem.

1. Discuss how verses 1–3 describe the countryside as night is falling:
   - pick out the words and phrases which tell you that it is getting dark
   - which sounds and movements in verse 1 suggest that the day is drawing to a close?
   - what sounds are described in verses 2 and 3? What mood is suggested by these sounds?

2. Pick out the details of the churchyard that are described in lines 13–14. What does the poet say about the village people who are buried there? What does this tell you about his view of them?

3. Imagine you have been asked to create a number of slides to be shown while someone is reading these verses. In pairs, discuss the photographs you would take and produce a picture-strip giving details of how you would illustrate each of the lines.

Notice how the *pace* and rhythm of this poem are used to help build up a picture of a day drawing to its close and a mood of reflection. In verse 1, for example, all the words are of either one or two *syllables* only. In pairs, practise a reading of the poem in order to put across the picture and the feeling that Gray creates.

The evening comes

About the poet

For details of Matthew Arnold see page 35.

About the poem

These lines describing the coming of evening are from a long poem called 'Bacchanalia; or The new age'. In the poem, Arnold describes how still the evening is after all the activity there has been in the fields during the day.

⁘⁓ The evening comes ⁓⁘

The evening comes, the fields are still.
The tinkle of the thirsty rill,
Unheard all day, ascends again;
Deserted is the half-mown plain,
Silent the swaths! the ringing wain,   5
The mower's cry, the dog's alarms,
All housed within the sleeping farms!
The business of the day is done,
The last-left haymaker is gone.
And from the thyme upon the height,   10
And from the elder-blossom white
And pale dog-roses in the hedge,
And from the mint-plant in the sedge,
In puffs of balm the night-air blows
The perfume which the day forgoes.   15

And on the pure horizon far,
See, pulsing with the first-born star,
The liquid sky above the hill!
The evening comes, the fields are still.

MATTHEW ARNOLD
(1822–88)

rill – stream
swaths – sheaves
wain – hay cart
sedge – coarse grass and rushes

Activities

Reading and writing

In pairs, read the poem, then write answers to these questions.

1. What sound can be heard now that evening has come?

2. What time of year is it? What sounds can be heard during the day?

3. List the plants and flowers that the poet says he can smell now that it is evening.

4. What impression of the evening sky is suggested by lines 16–18? What does the phrase 'liquid sky' tell us?

5. Can you think of another title for the poem? Give your reasons for suggesting it.

Write a poem in which, like Matthew Arnold, you describe sounds, movements and smells to create a picture of an evening scene. For example, you could describe the view from a bridge over a road or a river. Before you start writing your poem, list all the things you might include, then think about what impression you want to give of the scene, and underline the things on your list that will help you to create that impression.

Write a poem describing how a place is different at contrasting times of the day. For example, you could write about a railway station in the rush-hour and late in the evening after all the travellers have gone home or about a school playground in the daytime and in the evening.

Upon Westminster Bridge

About the poet

For details of William Wordsworth see page 80.

About the poem

This poem is a **sonnet** (see p. 24) with the **rhyme scheme** (see p. 19) *abba abba cdcdcd*. It was written a few weeks after Wordsworth and his sister Dorothy had crossed Westminster Bridge early one bright summer morning on board the coach from London to Dover.

Upon Westminster Bridge

Earth has not anything to show more fair:
    Dull would he be of soul who could pass by
    A sight so touching in its majesty:
This City now doth, like a garment, wear
The beauty of the morning; silent, bare,   5
    Ships, towers, domes, theatres, and temples lie
    Open unto the fields, and to the sky;
All bright and glittering in the smokeless air.
Never did sun more beautifully steep
    In his first splendour, valley, rock, or hill;   10
Ne'er saw I, never felt, a calm so deep!
    The river glideth at his own sweet will:
Dear God! the very houses seem asleep;
    And all that mighty heart is lying still!

WILLIAM WORDSWORTH
(1770–1850)

steep – soak completely

Activities

Reading and writing   In pairs, read the poem, then discuss these questions and write answers to them.

1. What does Wordsworth find impressive about the view he sees from Westminster Bridge? Which words and phrases suggest beauty and brightness?

2. Pick out the words and phrases that Wordsworth uses to describe the stillness.

3. Which of these words sum up how Wordsworth feels about the scene he sees:

    -   enchanted
    -   amazed
    -   surprised
    -   thrilled
    -   calmed?

    Give reasons for your views.

4. Remind yourself what a **metaphor** is (see p. 22) and pick out the metaphors which Wordsworth uses in the last two lines. What impression of the city do they give? What do the phrases 'seem asleep' and 'mighty heart' suggest?

Now write your own poem about a city scene. You could describe a quiet scene late at night or early in the morning or a bustling scene at mid-day or during the rush-hour.

The Hill Pines

About the poet

For details of Robert Bridges see page 77.

About the poem

Robert Bridges describes the felling of a 100-year-old oak tree. The poem is written in four-line verses which have the **rhyme scheme** (see p. 19) *abab*.

The Hill Pines

The hill pines were sighing,
O'ercast and chill was the day:
A mist in the valley lying
Blotted the pleasant May.

But deep in the glen's bosom 5
Summer slept in the fire
Of the odorous gorse-blossom
And the hot scent of the brier.

A ribald cuckoo clamoured,
And out of the copse the stroke 10
Of the iron axe that hammered
The iron heart of the oak.

Anon a sound appalling,
As a hundred years of pride
Crashed, in the silence falling: 15
And the shadowy pine-trees sighed.

ROBERT BRIDGES
(1844–1930)

odorous – strong smelling
brier – thorny shrub
ribald – abusive and mocking

Activities

Speaking and listening

In groups, discuss these questions. Keep notes of your ideas, then share them in a class discussion.

1. Talk about how Bridges uses the first verse to set the mood of the poem. What kind of day is described in verse 1? What mood does this conjure up?

2. Discuss how verse 2 provides a *contrast* with verse 1. Pick out the words and phrases which tell us what the glen will be like in summer.

3. Discuss how Bridges uses **alliteration** (see p. 2) and repetition in verse 3 to draw your attention to particular words. Which words indicate that the presence of the cuckoo in the wood is out of place? What do the words used to describe the sound of the axe suggest?

4. Talk about how the poet feels about the oak being felled. Which words and phrases in verse 4 tell you how he feels? Discuss how you feel about trees like the oak tree being cut down.

Creative writing   Write a poem to express your feelings about a conservation issue: for example, the pollution or destruction of part of the countryside. You could use a four-line verse form as Bridges does in 'The Hill Pines'. You could illustrate your poems and design them into posters to display around the school.

Meeting at Night

About the poet

Robert Browning was one of the leading Victorian poets. He ran away with and married Elizabeth Barrett (see p. 99). They lived in Italy for 15 years until her death. One of his most famous poems for younger people is 'The Pied Piper of Hamelin'.

About the poem

This poem describes a secret meeting between two lovers. It was written in 1845, the year before Browning and Elizabeth Barrett ran away together. Notice how Browning uses an unusual verse form and **rhyme scheme** (see p. 19) *abccba* to great effect.

Meeting at Night

The grey sea and the long black land;
And the yellow half-moon large and low;
And the startled little waves that leap
In fiery ringlets from their sleep,
As I gain the cove with pushing prow,   5
And quench its speed i' the slushy sand.

Then a mile of warm sea-scented beach;
Three fields to cross till a farm appears;
A tap at the pane, the quick sharp scratch
And blue spurt of a lighted match,   10
And a voice less loud, through its joys and fears,
Than the two hearts beating each to each!

ROBERT BROWNING
(1812–89)

prow – front of a boat

Activities

Reading and writing

In pairs, read the poem, then discuss the questions and write answers to them.

1. What details of the scene are you given in lines 1–4? What mood do these details suggest?

2. In the first eight lines, how does Browning indicate that the person is prepared to go to extremes to see their lover?

3. Which words and phrases suggest that the meeting is a secret one?

4. What indicates that the person's arrival is expected and eagerly awaited?

Imagine you have been asked to take some photographs to use as slides to be shown while someone reads the poem. In pairs, decide how many photographs you would take, then produce a picture-strip giving details of each photograph.

Write a poem describing the thoughts and feelings of a person waiting for their lover to arrive for a secret meeting.

In Prison

About the poet

William Morris was a poet, painter, designer and social reformer. He set up a manufacturing company to produce items such as furniture and wallpaper to try to replace ugly mass-produced articles with beautifully designed objects. His designs are still used on textiles and wallpaper today.

About the poem

This poem describes a knight's thoughts as he lies in prison.

In Prison

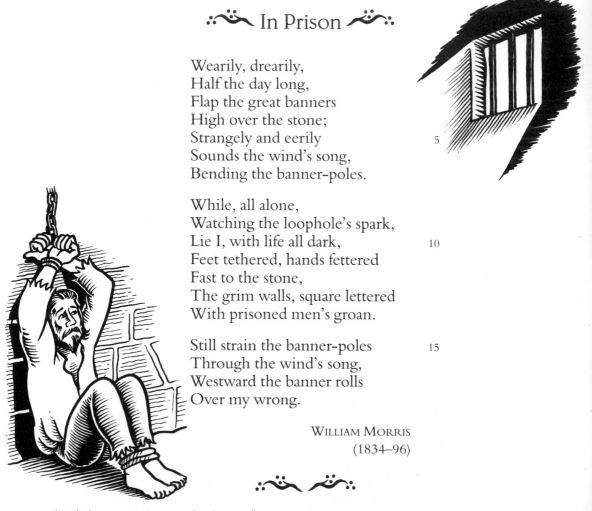

Wearily, drearily,
Half the day long,
Flap the great banners
High over the stone;
Strangely and eerily   5
Sounds the wind's song,
Bending the banner-poles.

While, all alone,
Watching the loophole's spark,
Lie I, with life all dark,   10
Feet tethered, hands fettered
Fast to the stone,
The grim walls, square lettered
With prisoned men's groan.

Still strain the banner-poles   15
Through the wind's song,
Westward the banner rolls
Over my wrong.

WILLIAM MORRIS
(1834–96)

loophole – a narrow opening in a wall

Activities

Speaking and listening

Discuss these questions in groups. Keep notes of your ideas, then share them in a class discussion.

1. Talk about the prison. List the details of the prison that are included in the poem. What kind of prison do you think it is?

2. Why do you think the person is in prison? What does 'my wrong' (line 18) suggest?

3. Discuss how in verse 1 Morris stresses the four *adverbs* by placing them before the verbs to which they refer. What do 'wearily, drearily' and 'strangely, eerily' convey about the prisoner's mood and what it feels like to be in that prison?

4. Talk about the prisoner's mood. Which of these words sums up what his mood is:

   - defiant
   - resigned
   - angry
   - despairing
   - hopeful?

   Can you think of any others? Give reasons for your answer.

In groups, talk about people who are put in prison for their political views. Are there any circumstances in which you would be prepared to go to prison rather than obey the law?

Creative writing

Imagine you are a political prisoner being held in solitary confinement. Write a letter, a diary entry or a poem describing your thoughts and feelings.

The Man He Killed

About the poet

For details of Thomas Hardy see page 61.

About the poem

Hardy imagines a man who has killed an enemy soldier thinking about the man he has killed and why he killed him. The poem is written as if the soldier is speaking his thoughts aloud.

The Man He Killed

'Had he and I but met
By some old ancient inn,
We should have sat us down to wet
Right many a nipperkin!

'But ranged as infantry,   5
And staring face to face,
I shot at him as he at me,
And killed him in his place.

'I shot him dead because –   10
Because he was my foe,
Just so: my foe of course he was;
That's clear enough; although

'He thought he'd 'list, perhaps,
Off-hand like – just as I –   15
Was out of work – had sold his traps –
No other reason why.

'Yes; quaint and curious war is!
You shoot a fellow down
You'd treat if met where any bar is,   20
Or help to half-a-crown.'

THOMAS HARDY
(1840–1928)

wet – drink
nipperkin – mug of ale
traps – to catch rabbits, etc., which he would sell for a living

Activities

Reading and writing
In pairs, read the poem and discuss these questions, then write answers to them.

1. In the first verse, what does the soldier say the two men might have done if they had met in a different way?

2. What do you learn in the second verse about why they shot at one another?

3. Which words and phrases in the third verse imply that the soldier is both puzzled and uncertain about what he has done?

4. What does the soldier tell us in the fourth verse about why he volunteered? What does the phrase 'off-hand like' suggest?

5. Why does he say war is 'quaint and curious' (line 17)?

6. How does he feel at the end of the poem? Do you think talking about the killing has helped him in any way?

7. What statement about war do you think Hardy is trying to make in this poem?

Speaking and listening   In pairs, discuss how Hardy writes as if someone is speaking. Pick out the points in the poem where the soldier pauses and hesitates, as if he is thinking and searching for what he wants to say. Discuss what sort of person you think the soldier is, then take it in turns to read the poem aloud and try to speak the lines as you think the soldier would speak them.

Creative writing   Write a poem in a similar style in which a person is thinking aloud about war and its consequences. For example, you could imagine you are someone who has just had their home destroyed in a bombing raid or a person who has just been told that one of their relatives has been killed in action. Try to write as if the person is speaking their thoughts aloud, as Hardy does, but do not worry about trying to make it rhyme, unless you want to do so.

From 'The Cry of the Children'

About the poet

Elizabeth Barrett Browning published her first book of poems when she was only 14. Her father was very strict and objected to his children getting married. So when Elizabeth fell in love with the poet Robert Browning, they got married in secret and ran away to Italy.

About the poem

These lines are from a political poem, 'The Cry of the Children', which was published in 1843. Elizabeth Barrett Browning wrote the poem after reading accounts of children working in mines and factories for up to 14 hours a day in very bad conditions.

From 'The Cry of the Children'

'For oh,' say the children, 'we are weary,
  And we cannot run or leap;
If we cared for any meadows, it were merely
  To drop down in them and sleep.
Our knees tremble sorely in the stooping,   5
  We fall upon our faces, trying to go;
And, underneath our heavy eyelids drooping,
  The reddest flower would look as pale as snow;
For, all day, we drag our burden tiring
  Through the coal-dark, underground –   10
Or, all day, we drive the wheels of iron
  In the factories, round and round.

'For all day the wheels are droning, turning;
  Their wind comes in our faces, –
Till our hearts turn, – our heads with pulses burning,   15
  And the walls turn in their places:
Turns the sky in the high window, blank and reeling,
  Turns the long light that drops adown the wall,
Turn the black flies that crawl along the ceiling:
  All are turning, all the day, and we with all.   20
And all day, the iron wheels are droning,
  And sometimes we could pray,
"O ye wheels," (breaking out in a mad moaning)
  "Stop! be silent for to-day!"'

ELIZABETH BARRETT BROWNING
(1806–61)

reeling – whirling about

Activities

Speaking and   In pairs, read the poem and discuss these questions before
listening   writing answers to them.

1. What do you learn from the first verse about what the
   children do all day? Which words and phrases tell you?

2. Which words and phrases in lines 1–8 suggest that the
   children are worn out?

3. What impression do you get of the factories from the second verse? Which details give you that impression?

4. Which words and phrases are repeated in the second verse? What does this repetition suggest first about the work the children have to do and second about the effect that the working conditions have on the children?

5. What plea do the children make in lines 22–4? Notice how **alliteration** (see p. 2) is used in line 23 to draw attention to the way the children say their prayer. What does the phrase 'mad moaning' suggest?

Speaking and listening In groups, prepare a reading of the poem. Work out a way of reading it so that you show how the children gradually get more and more tired from repeating the same actions hour after hour. Experiment with ways of varying the *pace* and volume of your reading in order to build towards a climax in the final three lines.

Creative writing Use the library to look for information about and illustrations of children working in the mines and factories and as chimney sweeps. Write your own poem about one of them and what their life is like.

The Slave's Dream

About the poet

Henry Wadsworth Longfellow was the most popular American poet of the nineteenth century. His epic poem, *The Song of Hiawatha*, sold over a million copies during his lifetime. He was the first American poet to be given a place in Poet's Corner in Westminster Abbey.

About the poem

This is one of seven poems on slavery which Longfellow wrote in 1842, 19 years before the outbreak of the American Civil War (1861–5) which led to slavery being abolished in the USA.

The Slave's Dream

Beside the ungather'd rice he lay,
    His sickle in his hand;
His breast was bare, his matted hair
    Was buried in the sand.
Again, in the mist and shadow of sleep,   5
    He saw his Native Land.

Wide through the landscape of his dreams
    The lordly Niger flowed;
Beneath the palm-trees on the plain   10
    Once more a king he strode;
And heard the tinkling caravans
    Descend the mountain road.

He saw once more his dark-eyed queen
    Among her children stand;
They clasp'd his neck, they kiss'd his cheeks,   15
    They held him by the hand! –
A tear burst from the sleeper's lids
    And fell into the sand.

And then at furious speed he rode
    Along the Niger's bank: 20
His bridle reins were golden chains,
    And, with a martial clank,
At each leap he could feel his scabbard of steel
    Smiting his stallion's flank.

Before him, like a blood-red flag,   25
    The bright flamingoes flew;
From morn till night he follow'd their flight,
    O'er plains where the tamarind grew,
Till he saw the roofs of Caffre huts,
    And the ocean rose to view.   30

At night he heard the lion roar,
    And the hyena scream,
And the river-horse, as he crush'd the reeds
    Beside some hidden stream;
And it pass'd, like a glorious roll of drums,   35
    Through the triumph of his dream.

The forests, with their myriad tongues,
    Shouted of liberty,
And the Blast of the Desert cried aloud,
    With a voice so wild and free,   40
That he started in his sleep and smiled
    At their tempestuous glee.

He did not feel the driver's whip,
    Nor the burning heat of day;
For Death had illumined the Land of Sleep,   45
    And his lifeless body lay
A worn-out fetter, that the soul
    Had broken and thrown away!

H.W. LONGFELLOW
(1807–82)

tinkling caravans – groups of traders
martial – warlike
scabbard – swordholder
smiting – striking
tamarind – a type of rice

Caffre – Kaffir (i.e. native African)
started – make a sudden movement
driver – overseer
fetter – chain fastened around ankle

Activities

In pairs, read the poem and discuss these questions, then write answers to them.

1. What does the first verse tell you about the slave and where he is lying? Why is the rice 'ungather'd'?

2. How is the life he dreams about in verses 2 and 3 different from the life he now lives? How does this make him feel?

3. What does he dream he is doing in verses 4 and 5? What details of his native land does he remember?

4. What sounds does he remember in verse 6? What does the last line of this verse suggest about his dream?

5. In verse 7 Longfellow uses **personification** (see p. 64) to suggest that in the slave's dream the forest and desert sounds become *symbols*. What are they symbols of? How does this make the slave feel? Which words and phrases indicate how he feels?

6. In verse 8 Longfellow tells us that the slave has died and uses a **metaphor** (see p. 22) to describe his lifeless body. Why does he compare the body to 'a worn-out fetter'? What does this suggest about the slave's death?

7. In your own words, sum up what this poem is about and what it tells you about Longfellow's attitude towards slavery.

Use the library to find out about the conditions in which slaves lived and worked in America. In addition to looking in reference books and history books, look out for books such as *To be a slave* and *Long Journey Home* by Julius Lester, *Underground to Canada* by Barbara Smucker and *The Slave Dancer* by Paula Fox.

Write a poem called 'The young slave' in which you describe the thoughts of a young girl or boy, either as they are on board a ship taking them away from their native land towards a life of slavery or as they work in the fields and wonder what it would have been like if they had been born and grown up in Africa.

Reflections

An emerald is as green as grass

About the poet

Christina Rossetti was born and lived her whole life in London. A devout Christian, she wrote mainly religious poetry.

About the poem

In this poem, Christina Rossetti reflects on the nature and value of various different types of stone. Before you read the poem, remind yourself what a **simile** is (see p. 12).

An emerald is as green as grass

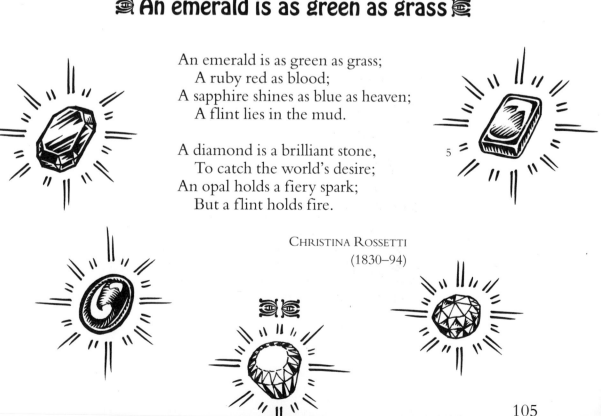

An emerald is as green as grass;
   A ruby red as blood;
A sapphire shines as blue as heaven;
   A flint lies in the mud.

A diamond is a brilliant stone,
   To catch the world's desire;
An opal holds a fiery spark;
   But a flint holds fire.

CHRISTINA ROSSETTI
(1830–94)

Activities

Speaking and listening   In pairs, discuss these questions. Make notes of your answers then share your ideas in a class discussion.

1. In the first verse, what similes does the poet use to make a contrast between the brightness of an emerald, a ruby and a sapphire and the dullness of a flint?

2. In the second verse, what does she say about the value of a diamond and an opal? How does she indicate that a flint is even more valuable?

3. In pairs, practise making up similes of your own by completing the following statements:

   - he was as angry as …
   - she ran as fast as …
   - it glittered as bright as …
   - the noise was as loud as …
   - the surface was as rough as …
   - its claws were as sharp as …
   - the floor was as slippery as …
   - the metal felt as cold as …

Creative writing   Try to write a poem of your own in which you include at least one simile. Either choose a subject of your own or write on one of the subjects from this list:

- clouds
- dusk
- fire
- footsteps
- fox
- volcano
- lake
- laughter
- bulldozer.

Imagine you have found a beautiful jewel. What does it look like? How do you feel as you hold it and examine it? Write a poem about it and try to include one or two similes to help you describe its appearance and how it makes you feel.

The Shepherd Boy's Song

About the poet

For details of John Bunyan see page 17.

About the poem

This poem is from *The Pilgrim's Progress*. Like a sermon, the poem puts across a message.

The Shepherd Boy's Song

He that is down needs fear no fall,
　He that is low, no pride;
He that is humble ever shall
　Have God to be his guide.

I am content with what I have,　　　　5
　Little be it or much:
And, Lord, contentment still I crave,
　Because Thou savest such.

Fullness to such a burden is
　That go on pilgrimage:　　　　10
Here little, and hereafter bliss,
　Is best from age to age.

JOHN BUNYAN
(1628–88)

Activities

Speaking and listening
Discuss these questions in pairs. Keep notes of your ideas, then share them in a group discussion.

1. Talk about how Bunyan suggests that life is a journey. List the words and phrases which imply that life is a journey.

2. Which words and phrases suggest that it is better to be content with what you have than to want too much?

3. Discuss each verse in turn and write a sentence summing up in your own words what Bunyan says in that verse.

4. It says in the Bible, 'Blessed are the meek, for they shall inherit the earth'. In which lines do you think Bunyan puts across this message most effectively? Do you agree with the message?

Creative writing
Write a poem or a story which puts across a message. You could try writing a song, as Bunyan does, or telling a story, as Robert Southey does in 'The Inchcape Rock' (see p. 29).

Lines Written on a Bank Note

About the poet

Robert Burns is Scotland's most famous poet. For most of his life he worked as a farmer. As well as poems, he wrote many songs, including 'Auld Lang Syne' and 'My Luv is like a Red Red Rose'. His birthday, 25 January, is known as Burns Night and many Scottish people celebrate by having a special dinner and singing some of Burns' songs.

About the poem

Burns wrote his poems in a Scottish *dialect*. This poem is written in **rhyming couplets** (see p. 4). Note that in the pronunciation of the dialect 'smile' (line 7) rhymes with 'spoil' (line 8) and 'wished' (line 9) rhymes with 'dust' (line 10).

🔁 Lines Written on a Bank Note 🔁

Wae worth thy power, thou cursēd leaf!
Fell source o' a' my woe and grief!
For lack o' thee I've lost my lass!
For lack o' thee I scrimp my glass!
I see the children of affliction   5
Unaided, through thy cursed restriction,
I've seen th' oppressor's cruel smile,
Amid his hapless victim's spoil,
And for thy potence vainly wished
To crush the villain in the dust.   10
For lack o' thee, I leave this much-loved shore,
Never, perhaps, to greet old Scotland more!

ROBERT BURNS
(1759–96)

🔁🔁

Wae worth – woe befall
Fell – deadly
For lack o' thee I scrimp my glass – for lack of money I have to reduce my drinking
children of affliction – children who are suffering
hapless – luckless
potence – the power money can buy

Activities

Reading and writing   Read the poem, then discuss these questions in pairs and write answers to them.

1. How does the person in the poem feel about the bank note? Which phrases in lines 1 and 2 tell you what he feels?

2. How has lack of money affected him (lines 3 and 4)?

3. Write down the words and phrases in lines 7 and 8 which suggest that rich people use money to take advantage of poor people.

4. Who is 'the villain' (line 10)? Which words and phrases (lines 9 and 10) indicate that the poet is feeling angry and powerless?

5. What does the person say he is going to have to do because of lack of money (lines 11 and 12)? How does he feel about having to do this?

6. In your own words, sum up the view of money that is put across in this poem.

Speaking and listening   In groups, talk about the different ways that people use money. Discuss how having money or not having money affects people's lives. Share your ideas in a class debate.

Creative writing   Write a poem of your own about money and its effects on people's lives. You could either use rhyming couplets, as Burns does, or find a form which you think suits the message you want to put across about money and its effects.

I Promise to pay the Bearer the sum of £5

Bredon Hill

About the poet

A.E. Housman was a classical scholar. Although he failed his degree at Oxford University, he later became Professor of Latin at University College, London. His most famous book of poems, *A Shropshire Lad*, was published in 1896.

About the poem

This poem tells a story of love and loss.

Bredon Hill

In summertime on Bredon
  The bells they sound so clear;
Round both the shires they ring them
  In steeples far and near,
  A happy noise to hear.   5

Here of a Sunday morning
  My love and I would lie,
And see the coloured counties,
  And hear the larks so high
  About us in the sky.   10

The bells would ring to call her
  In valley miles away;
'Come all to church, good people;
  Good people, come and pray.'
  But here my love would stay.   15

And I would turn and answer
  Among the springing thyme,
'Oh, peal upon our wedding,
  And we will hear the chime,
  And come to church in time.'   20

But when the snows at Christmas
  On Bredon top were strown,
My love rose up so early
  And stole out unbeknown
  And went to church alone.   25

They tolled the one bell only,
  Groom there was none to see,
The mourners followed after,
  And so to church went she,
  And would not wait for me.   30

The bells they sound on Bredon,
  And still the steeples hum.
'Come all to church, good people, – '
  Oh, noisy bells, be dumb;
  I hear you, I will come.   35

A.E. HOUSMAN
(1850–1936)

Activities

Read the poem, then in pairs discuss these questions and write answers to them.

1. What kind of sound does the poet suggest the church bells make in the first four verses of the poem? What do the lovers think of when they hear them?

2. What other sound is described in verse two? What mood does this sound convey?

3. In which verse do you first realise that this is going to be a sad story rather than a happy one? Explain why.

4. What do verses 5 and 6 tell you? Which line most clearly describes the lover's grief? Give reasons for your answer.

5. Compare the description of the noise of the bells in the last verse with how they are described in the first verse. What is the difference? Which words describe the difference?

6. How would you read the last line of the poem? What is the person who says these words feeling? Which of these words most accurately sums up how they are feeling:

   - despair
   - loneliness
   - resignation
   - bitterness
   - anger
   - anguish?

Give reasons for your answer.

Write a poem of your own which tells a story of love or loss. Before you begin, talk about how objects, creatures and sounds can be used as *symbols*. For example, the dove is a symbol of peace. Make a list of symbols and what they stand for, then when you write your poem try to choose a symbol which you can use to describe the feelings of happiness and/or sadness in the way that Housman uses the sound of church bells.

Country Sounds and Sights

About the poet

For details of John Clare see page 4.

About the poem

This is a list poem about sounds and sights in the countryside.

Country Sounds and Sights

The rustling of leaves under the feet in woods and under hedges;
The crumping of cat-ice and snow down wood-rides, narrow
    lanes, and every street causeway;
Rustling through a wood or rather rushing, while the wind halloos
    in the oak-top like thunder;   5
The rustle of birds' wings startled from their nests or flying unseen
    into the bushes;
The whizzing of larger birds overhead in a wood, such as crows,
    puddocks, buzzards;   10
The trample of robins and woodlarks on the brown leaves, and the
    patter of squirrels on the green moss;
The fall of an acorn on the ground, the pattering of nuts on the
    hazel branches as they fall from ripeness;
The flirt of the groundlark's wing from the stubbles – how sweet
    such pictures on dewy mornings when the dew flashes from its
    brown feathers!   15

JOHN CLARE
(1793–1864)

cat-ice – thin film of ice
puddocks – kites
flirt – quick movement

Activities

Speaking and listening Discuss these questions in pairs, make notes of your answers and then share your ideas in either a group or class discussion.

1. Talk about the words which Clare uses to describe the sounds of the countryside and make a list of them.

2. When writers describe a sound, they sometimes choose a word which actually imitates the sound they are describing. For example, words such as hiss, splash and murmur all suggest the sounds which they describe. The use of a word which echoes its meaning in its sound is called **onomatopoeia**.

   • Look at your list of the words which Clare uses. Find examples of words which imitate the sounds they are describing and underline those words.
   • Think of other examples of words which imitate the sounds they describe and make a list of them. For example, think of words that are used to describe animal noises, water sounds and the sound of machines.

3. In which line do you think Clare creates the clearest picture? Give reasons for your choice.

Creative writing Write your own list poem about sounds at night or school sounds. Before you begin decide what impression you want your list of sounds to create. Try to include some words which imitate the sounds they describe.

The Road Not Taken

About the poet

Robert Frost was an American poet who worked as a teacher and a farmer before becoming a full-time writer. He won the Pulitzer prize (the most important American poetry prize) four times and was invited to read a poem at the ceremony which followed the election of President Kennedy in 1961.

About the poem

In this poem, Frost describes two roads leading in different directions in order to suggest the choices people have to make in their lives.

The Road Not Taken

Two roads diverged in a yellow wood,
And sorry I could not travel both
And be one traveller, long I stood
And looked down one as far as I could
To where it bent in the undergrowth;   5

Then took the other, as just as fair,
And having perhaps the better claim,
Because it was grassy and wanted wear;
Though as for that the passing there
Had worn them really about the same,   10

And both that morning equally lay
In leaves no step had trodden black.
Oh, I kept the first for another day!
Yet knowing how way leads on to way,
I doubted if I should ever come back.   15

I shall be telling this with a sigh
Somewhere ages and ages hence:
Two roads diverged in a wood, and I –
I took the one less travelled by,
And that has made all the difference.   20

ROBERT FROST
(1875–1963)

diverged – separated after being one path
wanted wear – was less worn by travellers (i.e. still grassy)

Activities

**Reading and
writing** Discuss these questions in pairs and then write answers to them.

1. What do you learn about the two roads in the first two verses? In what ways are they similar?

2. What are the two different roads meant to represent?

3. How does the person in the poem feel about having to make a choice? Which words tell you that the choice was a difficult one?

4. Why did the person in the poem choose one road rather than the other?

5. Having made his choice, how did he feel? Pick out the words and phrases that tell you how he felt.

6. What is suggested in the line 'I shall be telling this with a sigh'?

7. Which line indicates that the choice of road influenced the person's whole life?

8. Why do you think Frost called the poem 'The Road Not Taken'? Do you think it is a suitable title? Explain why.

Write a story or a poem about a person faced with a difficult choice.

To Daffodils

About the poet

Robert Herrick was a Devonshire vicar. He is famous for his poems about nature and English country life and for the love lyrics he wrote to imaginary ladies.

About the poem

This poem consists of two ten-line verses, in which the lengths of each line vary from eight *syllables* to two syllables. Before reading the poem, remind yourself what a **simile** is (see p. 12).

To Daffodils

Fair daffodils, we weep to see
   You haste away so soon;
As yet the early-rising sun
   Has not attained his noon.
      Stay, stay
     Until the hasting day
      Has run
     But to the evensong;
And, having prayed together, we
   Will go with you along.   10

We have short time to stay as you,
   We have as short a spring;
As quick a growth to meet decay,
   As you, or anything.
      We die   15
     As your hours do, and dry
      Away
     Like to the summer's rain;
Or as the pearls of morning's dew,
   Ne'er to be found again.   20

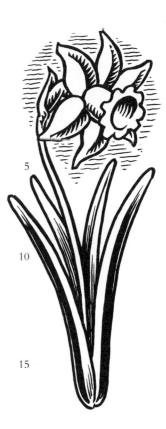

ROBERT HERRICK
(1591–1674)

attained – reached
evensong – evening church service

Activities

Reading and writing   Discuss these questions in pairs, then write answers to them.

1. In the first verse, Herrick reflects on the length of daffodils' lives. What are his feelings about how short their lives are? Which words and phrases tell you how he feels about the daffodils?

2. In the second verse, he reflects on the transience of human life. Which words and phrases in lines 11–14 stress how brief human lives are?

3. What two similes does Herrick use in lines 18 and 19 ? What do they suggest about people's lives?

4. Which of these words best sums up the mood of the poem:

- hopeful
- pensive
- sad
- melancholic
- despairing?

Give reasons for your answer.

Speaking and listening In pairs, take it in turns to practise reading the poem aloud. Before you begin, compare your answers to question 4 (above) and discuss what mood you want your reading of the poem to create.

The Old Men Admiring Themselves in the Water

About the poet

Yeats was an Irish poet, playwright and senator. He played an important part in setting up the famous Abbey Theatre in Dublin and in encouraging Irish culture and writing about Irish life. In 1923, he was awarded the Nobel Prize for Literature.

About the poem

This poem is about a number of old men who are sitting and looking at their reflections in the water. Before reading the poem, remind yourself what a **simile** is (see p. 12).

The Old Men Admiring Themselves in the Water

I heard the old, old men say,
'Everything alters,
And one by one we drop away.'
They had hands like claws, and their knees
Were twisted like the old thorn-trees   5
By the waters.
I heard the old, old men say,
'All that's beautiful drifts away
Like the waters.'

W.B. YEATS
(1865–1939)

Activities

Speaking and listening

In groups, discuss these questions. Make notes of your answers, then share your ideas in a class discussion.

1. Discuss what picture the old men see of themselves when they look in the water. What does the word 'admiring' in the title suggest?

2. Talk about what the poet sees when he looks at the old men. What similes does he use to describe their appearance in lines 6–8? What do they indicate about the old men?

3. How does what the poet says in lines 4–6 influence your view of what the old men say in lines 7–9?

4. Here are some statements about the poem. Say whether you agree or disagree with them and why:
   - the old men are afraid of death
   - the poet pities the old men
   - the old men are unable to see how age has affected their appearance.

Notice how the poet uses rhythm and rhyme to suggest the slow, but inevitable, passage of time. Almost all the words in the poem are of either one or two *syllables* and Yeats uses only three rhymes. In pairs, practise reading the poem aloud. Discuss what mood you want to create and how you can use the *pace* of the poem to create that mood.

There is no Frigate like a Book

🐢 There is no Frigate like a Book 🐢

There is no Frigate like a Book
To take us Lands away
Nor any Coursers like a Page
Of prancing Poetry –
This Traverse may the poorest take   5
Without oppress of Toll –
How frugal is the Chariot
That bears the Human soul.

EMILY DICKINSON
(1830–86)

🐢🐢

Frigate – sailing-ship
Coursers – swift horses
frugal – simple in needs
Chariot – body

Activities

Reading and writing   Read the poem, then discuss it in pairs and write answers to these questions.

1. Which words and phrases in the first four lines conjure up journeys and travelling?

2. What two similes does Emily Dickinson use in lines 1–4? What do they suggest happens to us when we read?

3. How do lines 5 and 6 indicate that the experience of reading is something that is open to everybody?

4. What do lines 7 and 8 tell us about people and their needs?

Write an entry for a reading journal about the experiences you have had reading, talking and writing about the poems in this collection. Say which poems are your favourites and explain why you like them.

Glossary

adverb: a word which helps to give more information about a verb or an adjective or another adverb. Many adverbs end in –ly. For example, 'She laughed *loudly*'.

comparison: (in poetry) a way of showing the likeness between two different things

contrast: to describe two things in order to show their differences.

dialect: a kind of English spoken in a particular area or by a particular group of people, which has its own words, grammar and pronunciation

image: a picture created in the mind by words and the ideas which they suggest

moral: the lesson about how to behave which can be learned from the events in a story or poem

pace: the rate of speed which the rhythm of a poem creates; also the rate of speed at which the lines of a poem are spoken

refrain: part of a song, such as a chorus, which is repeated regularly

stress: the emphasis put on a syllable (see below) by pronouncing it more firmly than a syllable which is not stressed

syllable: a unit of sound which forms a word or a part of a word. For example, 'hand' has one syllable, 'hand-some' has two syllables and 'hand-ker-chief' has three syllables

symbol: an object, person or idea which is used to stand for or suggest something else.

Index of poets

Index of first lines

Definitions

These terms are defined on the pages shown below and are cross-referenced throughout the book.